Embracing the Power of *Gratitude* Every Day

Thanks Living

STU EPPERSON JR.

FOREWORD BY DR. GARY CHAPMAN

#1 *NEW YORK TIMES* BESTSELLING AUTHOR OF *THE 5 LOVE LANGUAGES*®

MOODY PUBLISHERS
CHICAGO

All emphasis in Scripture has been added.

Names and details of some stories have been changed to protect the privacy of individuals.

Edited by Amanda Cleary Eastep
Interior Design: Puckett Smartt
Cover design: Graham Terry

ISBN: 978–0-8024–3889–8

Originally delivered by fleets of horse-drawn wagons, the affordable paperbacks from D. L. Moody's publishing house resourced the church and served everyday people. Now, after more than 125 years of publishing and ministry, Moody Publishers' mission remains the same—even if our delivery systems have changed a bit. For more information on other books (and resources) created from a biblical perspective, go to www.moodypublishers.com or write to:

Moody Publishers
820 N. LaSalle Boulevard
Chicago, IL 60610

1 3 5 7 9 10 8 6 4 2

Printed in the United States of America

CONTENTS

Dedication to "Big Stu"

Early on a summer Monday morning around four o'clock, our rock, our patriarch, our leader, our family shepherd—my dad, Stuart Epperson Sr.—came face-to-face with the Good Shepherd. I'll never forget how Mom responded to Pastor Will when he came by to pray with us. "Pastor," she replied, "all I can say is that I'm deeply grateful to God for the sixty amazing years He allowed me to be married to Stu. These were wonderful years—more than I ever deserved."

Her deep gratitude—rather than resentment—during the most difficult season of our lives, set in motion a stream of thanksgiving that flowed to thousands at the celebration service later that week and is still touching people today. All of our remembrances became thanksgiving celebrations of the goodness of God in the life of my dad, Big Stu.

Rather than throwing our anger at God for taking Dad "too soon" or becoming bitter and blaming, we experienced deep thankfulness. Yes, we shed a fountain of tears, but they welled up into a fountain of thankfulness pouring from our hearts. This fountain supernaturally touched many of the people who traveled from all over the world to pay their last respects and blessed untold numbers of those who watched online.[1]

One thing you need to understand about Dad is that he was a thankful man. Thankful that God saved him as a youth from bootlegging moonshine in the foothills of southwestern Virginia. Thankful that God turned him into one of the greatest evangelists of his generation through Christian media. He was thankful all the way to his last breath for a godly wife, children, grandchildren, and great-grandchildren.

There were times even during Dad's brutal chemo treatments that he would look at me and say, "Stuart, we have so much to be thankful for!" And he meant it. Then he'd hand me a gospel booklet to give the attending nurse. People full of thanksgiving are truly giving people. So many here on earth and already in heaven have received his generous gifts.

A family friend, Mark, texted me these kind words just after Dad passed: "Your dad bought me my first suit as an adult, saying, 'Everyone needs at least one good suit . . . and a blue blazer too!' Then later he shipped me to Bob Jones University, which ended up being life-changing!"

Dan, an accomplished attorney, shared: "Your dad was a great man. Way back when my parents couldn't afford to send me to camp, they told me Big Stu was covering it. I am now board chairman of an amazing camp that provides safe Christian camping to teens and Native Americans all over the West. We don't know, this side of heaven, the impact of our fruit. Now Big Stu gets to find out."

I'm still getting these kinds of calls and notes weekly.

My father saw thanksgiving as "thanks-*living*," and that's the driving passion of this book. Dad's gratitude and generosity inspired so many. He experienced Thanksgiving as much more than an annual, one-day event. In fact, the longer the Lord kept him with us, the more he modeled for us a daily "in everything give thanks" lifestyle. One of the beautiful things I've learned since his passing is that I don't have to follow him; I simply follow the One he followed—the Lord Jesus Christ.

You won't be surprised to hear that Dad loved to study, discuss, and share God's Word. He and Mom hosted, attended, taught, and facilitated all kinds of Bible study groups over the course of their sixty years of marriage—this is in addition to helping put some of the best Bible teachers on the radio. My prayer is that this book will honor and even expand his legacy as we look at a verse he loved and often quoted. He heard me teach and sing it many times at our Wednesday in the Word men's group at the local Dairi-O.

With or without hamburgers and ice cream, may this little book honor Big Stu, my hero, who leaves behind a lifetime of thanksgiving blessings that are being passed along to his wife, children, grandchildren, great-grandchildren, and spiritual children, now and for many generations to come.

Foreword

For the Christian, Thanksgiving is more than a holiday. It is meant to be a way of life. However, not all Christians have found this to be true in their own experience. Like non-Christians, they can give thanks when things are going well. But when disappointment enters their lives, they find it hard to give thanks.

Thanks-Living is a book dedicated to helping the reader develop a relationship with God and His Word that leads us to give thanks even when we don't understand our circumstances. Christianity, at its heart, is not a set of rituals we perform. It is a relationship with God our Father who loves us and is always with us.

At the heart of every relationship is communication: talking and listening. We develop our relationship with God by talking and listening to God. He speaks clearly to us in the Scriptures. We can talk openly with Him through prayer. Yes, we can share with Him our feelings of sadness, disappointment, or frustration, and feelings of happiness, excitement, etc. But thanksgiving is not an emotion. It is an attitude, a fixed way of thinking. It is a matter of the heart.

If we have a close relationship with God, we can give thanks in every situation regardless of our feelings. We know that even if our circumstances were caused by sinful behavior, God loves us and will work good out of it. He loves us and walks closely with us in the sunshine and the rain.

I'm grateful for this book by Stu Jr.; I've known his family for years. His dad, "Big Stu", was a wonderful friend who lived a life of genuine gratitude even in the face of declining health. He reminded us all by his life to be thankful in all things.

This book, if read thoughtfully and in close fellowship with God, will help you develop the biblical practice of thanks-living.

—Gary Chapman, PhD, author of The 5 Love Languages®

"Gratitude is a handmaiden of *contentment*. An ever-growing attitude of gratitude will certainly make us more content since we will be focusing more on what we do have, both spiritually and materially, than on what we do not have. But contentment is more than focusing on what we have. It is focusing on the fact that all we do have, we have by the grace of God. We do not deserve anything we have, materially or spiritually. It is all by His grace."

—Jerry Bridges[1]

CHAPTER 1

Thanks-Living: Why 5:18?

In everything give thanks: for this is the will of God in Christ Jesus for you.

1 THESSALONIANS 5:18

So many profound single verses from the Bible resound in our souls like a divine mic drop. We highlight, underline, memorize, and even sign these scriptural Mount Everests by our names. Yet how often do we miss the rich depths of their meanings?

First Thessalonians 5:18 is certainly one of these "one-verse wonders" that deserve a closer look. What if you found out that it meant a lot more, or even meant something completely different, than you always thought?

Studying it forced me to slow down and take in the full flavor of its meaning and place in God's Word. I've seen the 35,000-foot view for so many years. Yet all this time, I had no idea of the satisfying spiritual nutrients found in this amazing verse. Lord willing, after you get through the final page of this book you're holding, you should be able to do five important things.

1. You will have memorized an amazing verse.
2. You'll be able to meditate on—or mentally chew on—the Word of God, since you have committed this powerful verse to memory. Psalm 1:2 reminds us "his delight is in the law of the Lord, and in His law he meditates day and night."
3. You'll be able to teach others the deeper meaning of a rich Scripture verse. You'll have a new tool for one-on-one or group Bible study that will surely build others up in the Lord.
4. You'll be equipped with a powerful witnessing weapon to share with those around you who don't know Christ—who have no true reason for thanksgiving.
5. You'll have an affordable and portable resource to share as a gift.

In this book we'll closely consider each of the sixteen words that make up the five essential components of giving thanks found in 1 Thessalonians 5:18. They are:

- The amount
- The action
- The aim
- The access
- The application

These are the five A's of 5:18. Together they form the ingredients of a supernaturally satisfying Thanksgiving feast to be enjoyed every day of your life.

This is thanksgiving that transforms. The central focus of this verse is the gospel—the good news of what God has done for us, in Christ. We'll celebrate the perfect life, death, and resurrection of the Son of God who "loved me and gave Himself for me" (Gal. 2:20). He did for us what we could not do for ourselves. Apart from His giving, there is no cause for thanksgiving.

As we embark on this journey, we'll discover the richness of thanksgiving as a way of life—not just as a yearly holiday. Through a closer look at God's Word, we'll taste the intricate flavors of thankfulness, its source, and the joy it brings to our lives.

For too long, we've relegated the practice of thanksgiving to a holiday unobtrusively stuck between Halloween and Christmas. Thanksgiving was actually the first federal holiday declared in the United States. On October 3, 1789, President George Washington issued a proclamation naming Thursday, November 26, 1789, as an official holiday of "sincere and humble thanks." This day was not set apart for the people to make requests and petitions of God for our young nation with all kinds of issues. It was not to be a day of getting more from the Divine. In fact, Abraham Lincoln's decision to declare the fourth Thursday in November as the first annual federal holiday for Thanksgiving was during the Civil War - an important example of giving thanks during difficulties! Our founders saw the great need to give more thanks to God—and eventually they changed the entire calendar with this focus.

Tragically, this fourth Thursday of November has all too often been seen as merely an annoying delay before people can enjoy their yuletide celebrations. And yet, what would Christmas be without the giving of thanks? Christ came to us in the humility of the manger to save us from sin and death. Is there anything greater to be thankful for? Maybe we've got these two holidays in the wrong order. Either way, it's time to reorder our perspective, not by setting up a new calendar, but by resetting our hearts to be a daily calendar of thanks to God.

Thanksgiving is so much more than a feast we indulge in, the one day of the year we kick our diets to the curb. Trust me, no one loves Mama's homemade sweet potato casserole more than I do! But what about the far more satisfying and eternal "taste and see that the Lord is good" (Ps. 34:8) component to Thanksgiving? The "one-verse wonder" of 5:18 really is a "one-verse feast." So why wait until Thursday night when the food coma finally lifts? Let's redeem the Thanksgiving table all day and all year long![2]

Many of our neighbors are rediscovering the blessings of gratitude, even if many of them haven't yet discovered its source. According to the Pew Research Center, 78 percent of Americans feel a strong sense of gratitude or thankfulness on a weekly basis. Only 6 percent say they seldom or never experience gratitude.[3]

Robert Emmons, believed to be the world's leading scientific expert on gratitude, says that study after study confirms the absolute necessity of thankfulness in living a good life. Emmons, a professor of psychology at the University of California, Davis, and the founding editor in chief of *The Journal of Positive Psychology*, notes an undeniable link between gratitude and life satisfaction.[4]

Emmons consistently sees the following benefits of gratitude in the people he studies:

Physical

- Stronger immune systems
- Less bothered by aches and pains
- Lower blood pressure
- Exercise more and take better care of their health
- Sleep longer and feel more refreshed upon waking

Psychological

- Higher levels of positive emotions
- More alert, alive, and awake
- More joy and pleasure
- More optimism and happiness

Social

- More helpful, generous, and compassionate
- More forgiving
- More outgoing
- Feel less lonely and isolated[5]

Emmons believes that gratitude has two parts. First, he says, "it's an affirmation of goodness. We affirm that there are good things in the world, gifts and benefits we've received."[6] Second, he notes, "we recognize that the sources of this goodness are outside of ourselves. . . . We acknowledge that other people—or even higher powers, if you're of a spiritual mindset—gave us many gifts, big and small, to help us achieve the goodness in our lives."[7]

Health expert Dr. Mark Hyman says, "Gratitude is the ultimate biohack. It reduces stress, improves sleep, strengthens your immune system, and even aids digestion. The vagus nerve connects your brain and gut, gratitude activates it, calming your system. A grateful heart is essential for health."[8]

From "TED-talkers" to therapists, gratitude is being touted as an antidote, healer, and even a superpower.

Biloxi, Reno, and Atlantic City

What do Biloxi, Reno, and Atlantic City have in common? Yes, gambling is a big hit in all three cities. The food's not bad, either! But for our family, this is where we spent three interesting Thanksgivings while one of my daughters performed three consecutive years in big Christmas productions. During these memorable events in our lives, we met a whole lot of folks—many of whom didn't understand the real meaning of the holiday.

There's something heartbreaking about being in a massive casino on Thanksgiving Day, surrounded by a sea of people. We walked by aisle after aisle of slot machines, blackjack tables, and crowds of folks hopelessly drowning in their empty pursuit of happiness. I'll never forget one older gentleman with whom we were able to share the gospel. He was a father and grandfather.

How sad that instead of being with his family on Thanksgiving Day, he was gambling. I remember talking with him about the hope of the gospel while watching the Cowboys play on a screen bigger than a house. We shared how Jesus Christ alone could fill the emptiness in our souls and bring healing to his family if he would turn to Christ and trust the gospel. He listened and seemed touched by being around a family that cared about him and spoke with him.

In that moment, something heavy hit my heart. Rather than complain about not being with our extended family celebrating Thanksgiving as in most years, I became deeply grateful to the Lord. He has done so much for me to save me and bless me with a wonderful wife and family.

At the same time, I was also deeply convicted about all the times I took for granted many Thanksgivings surrounded by family. How eternally tragic to think that someone, perhaps even the lost gentleman before me, could walk out of that casino with a million dollars in winnings, hop into a limo, and yet still be completely empty in his soul!

Thanksgiving takes us deeper into areas of the soul that can't be bought or gambled for. It takes us into the things that really matter in life and eternity. If you've found true peace with God, you can thank Him in a casino or even in a Nazi prison camp, like Dietrich Bonhoeffer, who said,

> You must never doubt that I'm traveling with gratitude and cheerfulness along the road where I'm being led. My past life is brim-full of God's goodness, and my sins are covered by the forgiving love of Christ crucified. I'm so thankful for the people I have met, and I only

> hope that they never have to grieve about me, but that they, too, will always be certain of and thankful for God's mercy and forgiveness.[9]

So pause, take a deep breath, and let's journey together down the path of gratitude. First, we'll set the Thanksgiving table; then we'll take a closer look at the five A's of 5:18. What a thrill to allow God's Word to inspire us to give thanks in all circumstances, for this is God's will in Christ Jesus concerning us.

Discussion Questions for Chapter 1

1. What's my favorite verse that I've never really studied?
2. Why is it important to look closer at each verse in the Bible?
3. Why is Thanksgiving more than just an event or season?
4. Whom do I consider a thankful person? Why?

Living Thanks . . . Write It Down

5. What has this chapter inspired me to record in my gratitude journal?
6. To whom can I write a thank-you for helping me grow closer to God?
7. Whom can I call today just to "thank you"?

"Be thankful. God has commanded it—for our good and for His glory. God's command to be thankful is not the threatening demand of a tyrant. Rather, it is the invitation of a lifetime—the opportunity to draw near to Him at any moment of the day."

Nancy DeMoss Wolgemuth[1]

CHAPTER 2

Setting the 5:18 Table

We give thanks to God always for you all, making mention of you in our prayers, remembering without ceasing your work of faith, labor of love, and patience of hope in our Lord Jesus Christ in the sight of our God and Father.

1 Thessalonians 1:2–3

There wasn't a lot of feasting going on for Corrie ten Boom at the height of the Holocaust. During the Second World War, Corrie and her sister Betsie were taken captive and were living in a German concentration camp. In their barracks, they had organized a Bible study for the other women. One time, as Providence would have it, they were studying 1 Thessalonians 5:16–18: "In everything give thanks; for this is the will of God in Christ Jesus for you."

In discussing the application for these verses, Betsie said they should give thanks right there in the prison camp. She believed they should give thanks even for the *fleas*. Corrie was not having any of it. Yet Betsie insisted, and so in faith and obedience they gave thanks for the pesky fleas and even the awful lice.

A few weeks went by, and the ladies began to realize that no guards ever came into their barracks. No one interrupted their Bible studies. They wondered why, as other barracks faced constant harassment. One day Betsie overheard some guards refusing to go into her barracks. Why? The place was filled with fleas and lice. Now they saw God's purpose for the fleas—to protect them.[2]

Just as location, location, location are the three rules of real estate, it's context, context, context when studying God's Word. Rather than parachute in out of nowhere and miss the point of this meaningful verse, let's look at the context and setting of 1 Thessalonians 5:18. After all, don't we hear this verse a lot every Thanksgiving? We bring it up, cite it, write it, post it, and share it. It's a verse many of us have memorized. Our Bible apps push it to our mobile devices before we can even preheat the oven. How often have we gone around the Thanksgiving table referencing 5:18 and sharing what we're thankful for?

This is exactly why I've enjoyed drilling deeper and mining the rich golden nuggets contained in this profound little verse. I'm so glad to invite you along for the journey!

Get ready to study it, memorize it, meditate on it, teach it, enjoy it, live it, and even sing it—I think you'll love the 5:18 song "In Everything

Give Thanks." It's a memorable way to recount the important words of 1 Thessalonians 5:18.

Welcome to Thessaloniki

Who was the first to hear the rich words of 1 Thessalonians 5:18? Paul wrote this letter to a young, growing church in Thessaloniki, with a deep heart of gratitude. All five chapters are dripping with thanksgiving. He opens the book with these words: "We give thanks to God always for you all, making mention of you in our prayers, remembering without ceasing your work of faith, labor of love, and patience of hope in our Lord Jesus Christ in the sight of our God and Father" (1:2–3).

He continues with even more words of effusive gratitude: "For this reason we also thank God without ceasing, because when you received the word of God which you heard from us, you welcomed it not as the word of men, but as it is in truth, the word of God, which also effectively works in you who believe" (2:13). And, "For what thanks can we render to God for you, for all the joy with which we rejoice for your sake before our God" (3:9).

Written primarily in a tone of relief and gratitude, 1 Thessalonians is marked by Paul's thankfulness over the growth of the church during his forced absence. The letter contains no elaborate theology as Romans does, no rebuke of a threatening heresy as in Galatians, no extensive pastoral counsels such as in 1 Corinthians.[3] If ever there was a "Thanksgiving letter" in the Bible, this was it!

How is being ever-joyful and ever-prayerful related to being ever grateful? In the fifth chapter of 1 Thessalonians (where verse 18 appears), we find more than a dozen other punchy imperatives (see verses 11–22), exhorting this baby church.

What's going on in Thessaloniki? This church of young believers was on fire for Christ. Acts 17 records the apostle Paul's first experience in this thriving coastal Greek city where both Jews and Gentiles came to faith. Not only were they on fire, but they were also "under fire" for their newfound belief in Christ. The pagan Greek culture was not at all friendly to this new exclusive "one way to heaven" group of Jesus followers. Christians were to become known as "atheists" because they denied the existence of the gods of Olympus. On the other side, the Jewish community was turning up the heat as well. These same forces drove Paul, Silas, and Timothy out of town; they barely escaped with their lives (Acts 17:1–9).

Another characteristic of these Thessalonian believers is that they longed for the return of Christ. They were concerned with the big question, "When is Jesus Christ coming back?" In five encouraging chapters, Paul praises them, challenges them, and comforts them. He effectively says, "Hey, don't be discouraged. He's coming." No matter how evil and tough it gets, the Lord will return. He's going to split that eastern sky and come back through the clouds to rule and reign.

The risen Jesus that Paul preached is not coming back the way He arrived the first time. He won't return as a cute, cuddly little baby in a manger—as we celebrate at Christmas. He's not appearing the second time as the teacher who healed or the servant who suffered. He's returning as the omnipotent, conquering monarch. He'll arrive with the flaming sword of the Word of God out of His mouth and eyes like fire, as we read in Revelation:

> His head and hair were white like wool, as white as snow, and His eyes like a flame of fire; His feet were like fine brass, as if refined in a furnace, and His voice as the sound of many waters; He had in His right hand seven stars, out of His mouth went a sharp two-edged sword, and His countenance was like the sun shining in its strength. And when I saw Him, I fell at His feet as dead. But He laid His right hand on me, saying to me, "Do not be afraid; I am the First and the Last." (Rev. 1:14–17)

This is who's coming back. This is our returning King. Paul reminds these embattled saints in Thessaloniki that their King will return in triumph. Ready yourselves, for He will come quickly. To challenge them further, he says in 1 Thessalonians 5:2–6:

> For you yourselves know perfectly that the day of the Lord so comes as a thief in the night. For when they say, "Peace and safety!" then sudden destruction comes upon them, as labor pains upon a pregnant woman. And they shall not escape. But you, brethren, are not in darkness, so that this Day should overtake you as a thief. You are all sons of light and sons of the day. We are not of the night nor of darkness. Therefore let us not sleep, as others do, but let us watch and be sober.

Then Paul exhorts them to "comfort each other and edify one another" (v. 11). These words set up multiple familiar imperative challenges—all grounded in thanksgiving! A book could be written about each of these blessed exhortations. We'll focus on a few of them.

To rightly understand the *imperatives* of verses 5:11–22, we must understand the *indicatives* of verses 9–10: "For God did not appoint us to wrath, but to obtain salvation through our Lord Jesus Christ, who died for us, that whether we wake or sleep, we should live together with Him."

Simply put, the indicatives of Scripture remind us of what He's done *for* us and what He has done *in* us. Imperatives instruct us on how we respond now that He lives in and through us. It's important to get these in the right order since we can never perform our way into God's favor. Rather, we respond to His perfect performance by the power of His grace. As my pastor friend reminds me: "Imperatives without indicatives are impossibilities."

The rich indicatives of Christ's work for them and in them bookend all of the imperatives in chapter 5. Because of these Christians' union and position in Christ, Paul simply is calling them to live out what Jesus had already poured into them. None of us has the power to follow His commands apart from the power of the indwelling Holy Spirit. Later in chapter 5, verses 23 and 24 further punctuate God's mighty work in us:

> Now may the God of peace Himself sanctify you completely; and may your whole spirit, soul, and body be preserved blameless at the coming of our Lord Jesus Christ. He who calls you is faithful, who also will do it.

From their position of being fully accepted in Christ, Paul then tells these Christians to "warn those who are unruly, comfort the fainthearted, uphold the weak, be patient with all" (v. 14). "See that no one renders evil for evil to anyone, but always pursue what is good both for yourselves and for all" (v. 15). And then verses 16–18 give us the trifecta—three big, heart-driven responses to the gospel: "Rejoice always, pray without ceasing, in everything give thanks; for this is the will of God in Christ Jesus for you."

Rejoice Always

First, there's "rejoice always" (1 Thess. 5:16). What does it mean to always rejoice? To always have joy is to be full of joy. It's to have the same joy of the Lord about which the prophet Nehemiah spoke: "The joy of the LORD is your strength" (Neh. 8:10). This is a divinely deposited joy from God—an inner joy.

While happiness may often be based on "happenings," this true, heartfelt joy comes from being anchored in Jesus Christ. Rejoicing is joy in action. Paul uses essentially the same language in Philippians 4:4, where he says, "Rejoice in the Lord always. Again, I will say, rejoice!" True joy is always *in the Lord*. It's our humble response to His work in us. Joy only comes from Him. Yes, God wants us to be happy—but with a happiness in Him, that can only come from Him.

I like John Piper's definition: "Christian joy is a good feeling in the soul, produced by the Holy Spirit, as he causes us to see the beauty of Christ in the word and in the world."[4]

My wife, Julie, and I are blessed to have a daughter named Joy. Here is a good little acronym for Joy: *Jesus, others, you*. When you get the order right, you will have joy. And it won't be some glib, artificial experience, but a joy of deep, authentic strength. There might even be tears flowing from your eyes when you have true joy. And the Word tells us to rejoice just as often as we are to pray and give thanks—always.

Joy is also the second fruit of the Spirit after love in Galatians 5:22. Joy supernaturally springs forth in the life of the believer who is living under the control of the Holy Spirit. Walking in the Spirit is walking in joy. Jesus said, "These things I have spoken to you, that My joy may remain in you, and that your joy may be full" (John 15:11).

This is an ongoing, never-ending joy because His work in us is ongoing and never-ending. Joy is closely connected to prayer and ultimately to thanksgiving. Joy motivated Him all the way from the cradle to the cross to the crown: "Looking unto Jesus, the author and finisher of our faith, who for the joy that was set before Him endured the cross, despising the shame, and has sat down at the right hand of the throne of God" (Heb. 12:2).

Pray Without Ceasing

After "Rejoice always," Paul calls the Thessalonian Christians (and us) to "pray without ceasing" (1 Thess. 5:17).

Not only are we to be ever rejoicing, but ever praying. This is as much an attitude as it is an act of prayer. Prayer flows from a heart changed by the gospel. Prayer recognizes the "Lord is at hand" (Phil. 4:5) even when anxiety is in the air and the world is going crazy.

Does "pray without ceasing" mean we walk around like zombies with our eyes closed, bumping into people while voicing Gregorian chants? Not at all. It's an ongoing communication, like breathing, something we only think about when it's brought to our attention. Is uninterrupted prayer really possible? According to one commentator, the answer is yes and no: "In the Christian life the act of prayer is intermittent, but the spirit of prayer should be incessant."[5] This means taking our prayer life more seriously, walking with God, and listening to His voice.

There are also those rich, concentrated times where we get alone with the Father and pray without being distracted. Right in the middle of a major teaching and healing crusade when the demands of the world were upon Jesus, "Now in the morning, having risen a long while before daylight, He went out and departed to a solitary place; and there He prayed" (Mark 1:35). Another time, the Lord dismissed a huge crowd and sent His disciples off in a boat: "And when He had sent them away, He departed to the mountain to pray" (Mark 6:46).

How remarkable that, later on, His disciples didn't ask Jesus to teach them to preach, cast out demons, or walk on water. They asked Him to "teach us to pray" (Luke 11:1). Are you busier than Jesus was? Are you more important? Since we must answer no, let's make prayer a bigger priority.

The disciples were firsthand witnesses of Jesus' always rejoicing, unceasing prayer, and ever thankfulness. All three are inextricably related. Praying without ceasing enables one to rejoice always. This injunction should not be unduly pressed. We are not expected to abandon our tasks, duties, and times of rest in order to devote our lives to the one exercise of communion with God. Nor yet is it to be minimized to mean merely that one should cultivate a habit of prayer. Life, instead, is to be lived in a continual spirit of worship.

> Beneath the stream of thought there should flow the deep current of unconscious communion with God and the sense of his presence, a current ever and again rising into conscious petition and adoration and praise. One who thus lives will naturally and necessarily obey the command, "In everything give thanks." This is not only to express gratitude for everything, although that should be done, but also to "give thanks" under all conditions and in all circumstances.[6]

Worship is another rich word that encompasses this call to prayer. It simply means "ascribing worth" back to God.[7] We worship in so many ways beyond simply entering a sanctuary on Sundays at 11 a.m. Worship is a lifestyle expressed in word and deed, song and play, and work and life. Our whole life is simply to be an expression of worship to our great King because He alone is worthy. When we limit worship to an act or day of the week, we miss the whole point. As Paul reminds us, worship and thanksgiving are to characterize our whole lives. "And whatever you do in word or deed, do all in the name of the Lord Jesus, giving thanks to God the Father through Him" (Col. 3:17).

Constant prayer and rejoicing will inevitably flow into thanksgiving. Charles Spurgeon is believed to have said, "When joy and prayer are married, their first-born child is gratitude." Of course, we should be cautious when saying *always* and *every*. But thank God, prayer, rejoicing, and thanksgiving are wonderful exceptions. We must pray about every situation, no matter how small, no matter how unfruitful it might seem

(Phil. 4:6–7; Eph. 6:18). Pray about a difficult relationship, an interview for a job, a new opportunity, whatever.

Yes, God already knows. Yes, God cares about the situation. But did you pray about it? Do you pray about your struggles, or are you seeking only secular advice? Why would we go to TV sitcoms and scroll on social media when believers are encouraged to "come boldly to the throne of grace, that we may obtain mercy and find grace to help in time of need" (Heb. 4:16)? We can enter the very presence of Almighty God with any need and with no roaming charges! We can go to Jesus, our Wonderful Counselor, and pray to Him for all things, all the time, every time.

To pray in every single thing, no matter how big or small, also means going to God *first.* All of us need to take stock with some honest questions. Is prayer my first response or my last resort? Am I trusting in email or "knee-mail"? Praying without ceasing exposes one of the greatest enemies of prayer: pride. Prayer undermines our deeply rooted pride and self-sufficiency. Prayer debunks the belief that I can do it on my own. You may be a very capable person, but in John 15:5, Jesus reminds us that "without Me you can do nothing."

If you ask a room full of believers to raise their hand if they "pray enough," the response is predictable. None of us would dare say our prayer life is where it should be. But here's a simple reason for that—not to add guilt, but to address hunger. Yes, there are obvious issues of sin and laziness or growing callous over time. But when you get down to it, the reason we don't pray enough is because we can *never* get enough of God! He is so big and beautiful beyond our thoughts and imaginations. He welcomes us into His presence. The more time you spend with Him, the more time you want to spend with Him. Only God can satisfy our deepest hunger. Only in heaven will we begin to fully satisfy our hunger for God, uninterrupted by sin.

The psalmist describes it this way:

> You will show me the path of life;
> In Your presence is fullness of joy;
> At Your right hand are pleasures forevermore. (Ps. 16:11)

Prayer is also serious about spiritual warfare. Paul notes that we are to be "praying always" in Ephesians 6:18, the famous "armor of God" passage. How often do we teach this classic spiritual warfare passage on "suiting up" as a believer, but fail to go to the next verse that reveals the great weapon of prayer? Here is the passage in full:

> Finally, my brethren, be strong in the Lord and in the power of His might. Put on the whole armor of God, that you may be able to stand against the wiles of the devil. For we do not wrestle against flesh and blood, but against principalities, against powers, against the rulers of the darkness of this age, against spiritual hosts of wickedness in the heavenly places. Therefore take up the whole armor of God, that you may be able to withstand in the evil day, and having done all, to stand.
>
> Stand therefore, having girded your waist with truth, having put on the breastplate of righteousness, and having shod your feet with the preparation of the gospel of peace; above all, taking the shield of faith with which you will be able to quench all the fiery darts of the wicked one. And take the helmet of salvation, and the sword of the Spirit, which is the word of God; praying always with all prayer and

> supplication in the Spirit, being watchful to this end with all perseverance and supplication for all the saints. (Eph. 6:10–18)

You can have a shiny coat of armor, but if there's nothing inside, what good will it be in the rage of battle? Want to really enter the battle? Engage in intercessory prayer. Pray for others. Pray for lost souls. Pray for boldness. Pray for open doors to share the gospel.

Prayer takes the shiny body of armor out of the great hall of display and into the flaming heat of the battle. This is exactly what Paul asked the church at Ephesus to do; to pray for him "that utterance may be given to me, that I may open my mouth boldly to make known the mystery of the gospel, for which I am an ambassador in chains; that in it I may speak boldly, as I ought to speak" (Eph. 6:19–20).

In Everything Give Thanks

Paul connected prayer and thanksgiving even in intercession for other saints, saying, "We give thanks to the God and Father of our Lord Jesus Christ, praying always for you" (Col. 1:3). And to his son in the faith, Timothy, he said, "I thank God, whom I serve with a pure conscience, as my forefathers did, as without ceasing I remember you in my prayers night and day" (2 Tim. 1:3).

Matthew Henry further demonstrates how 5:18 flows. He shows the strong interconnectedness of perpetual prayer and gratitude.

> *In every thing give thanks*, v. 18. If we pray without ceasing . . . we must not omit thanksgiving, Phil. 4:6. We should be thankful in every condition, even in adversity as well as prosperity. It is never so bad with us but it might be worse. If we have ever so much occasion to make our

> humble complaints to God, we never can have any reason to complain of God, and have always much reason to praise and give thanks: the apostle says, This is the *will of God in Christ Jesus concerning us, that we give thanks,* seeing God is reconciled to us in Christ Jesus; in him, through him, and for his sake, he allows us to rejoice evermore, and appoints us in every thing to give thanks. It is pleasing to God.[8]

Paul's passionate instructions to this church are not one-offs or Sunday-only activities. These are marks of redeemed saints who are bound toward heaven and eagerly awaiting the blessed hope—the second coming of King Jesus. Each of these pithy exhortations flows out of deep gratitude to the indwelling Christ—the One they longed to meet—either by death or by His soon return. The finished work of Jesus on their behalf was the basis for ongoing joy, prayer, and thanksgiving. These aren't necessarily events, transactions, appointments, or a box we check. Rather they are fluid lifelines for these who have been redeemed. This is a Thanks Living. These encouraging words set the table and provide the context for the main thanksgiving course of 5:18.

Only by God's Power

The entire epistle reminds us that it's only by God's power working in us that we can experience such joy, prayer, and thanksgiving—through the gospel of Jesus Christ.

> Obedience to these commands is difficult. Indeed, it may seem impossible. However, a ringing word of encouragement is added: "for this is the will of God in Christ Jesus for you." That we should

> lead lives of continual joy, of ceaseless prayer, of constant thanksgiving, is not merely the desire, the expectation, the command of God; it is His purpose, His will, and therefore is certain to be fulfilled. This ideal has been realized in Christ, and it is in His power, and in virtue of His indwelling, that such an ideal will be realized with increasing perfection by those who trust and follow him.[9]

Whether it's your family feasting during the holiday or Corrie ten Boom and her sister being flea-bitten during the Holocaust, these rich verses remind us to be ever joyful, ever prayerful, and always thankful. Why? Because the King has come.

And aren't you thankful that the King is coming again?

Discussion Questions for Chapter 2

1. Why is the context of 1 Thessalonians 5:18 so important?
2. What's my favorite thanksgiving verse in the Bible?
3. Why is prayer such an important part of the armor of God?
4. How is my rejoicing and praying connected with thanksgiving?

Living Thanks . . . Write It Down

5. What has this chapter inspired me to record in my gratitude journal?
6. To whom can I write a thank-you note today for praying for me during a difficult season?

"We ought to give thanks for all fortune: if it is good, because it is good, if bad, because it works in us patience, humility and the contempt of this world and the hope of our eternal country."

C. S. Lewis[1]

CHAPTER 3

The Amount— "In Everything"

Blessed be the name of the LORD
From this time forth and forevermore!
From the rising of the sun to its going down
The LORD's name is to be praised.

PSALM 113:2–3

Gary and Karolyn Chapman were a gifted young couple who thought they were on their way to fulfilling their dream of training missionaries all over the world. One thing stood between them and their calling—a doctorate. Three years later, with diploma in hand, the mission board turned this young couple down. Gary and Karolyn were shocked and heartbroken. But they trusted the Lord and gave thanks anyway.

Little did they know that, decades later, Dr. Gary Chapman's most popular book, *The 5 Love Languages*, would sell over twenty million copies in English, be translated into fifty other languages, and consistently appear on the *New York Times* bestsellers list, sometimes claiming the #1 spot.[2]

The immense impact of Gary's books globally will only be fully reported in heaven.

Recently, my close friend and mentor of many years, David Parsons, had what he thought was a minor irregular heartbeat. After over a week in the hospital, he was diagnosed with a serious condition that called for immediate open-heart surgery. During this ordeal, David and his family would face some of the toughest days and weeks of their lives. Yet his attitude of thanksgiving was still very real. David put dozens of sticky notes with Bible verses all over his hospital room and described his commitment this way:

> "I read the promises of the Son of God and believe that the person Jesus Christ has paid all our sin and rescued us to Himself. I printed and pasted these promises on the hospital door. Calling to remembrance the promises of God, that He took my place and the person of Jesus Christ gives me a thankful heart. He never has and never will fail. I can have Thanksgiving as I trust Him."
>
> The Word says that God inhabits the praises of His people (Psalm 22:3). It's amazing to think that God, in all His fullness, inhabits and dwells in our praises of Him. Our praise is irresistible to God. As soon as He hears us call His name, He is ready to answer us.[3]

An Ongoing Attitude

Whether it's a clean bill of health from the doc or a sudden call for triple bypass surgery, we are to give thanks "in everything." Some translations read "in all circumstances." Many other Scriptures call us to a life of thanksgiving. For example:

- "Be thankful to Him, and bless His name" (Ps. 100:4).
- "Offer to God thanksgiving, and pay your vows to the Most High" (Ps. 50:14).
- "Be anxious for nothing, but in everything by prayer and supplication, with thanksgiving, let your requests be made known to God" (Phil. 4:6).

Just like the perpetual nature of unceasing prayer and evermore rejoicing, thanksgiving is an ongoing attitude for the child of God. Since nothing happens by chance, there's an opportunity for thanks in everything.

A moment's reflection, however, reminds us that "in" does not necessarily mean "for." Consider the members of a family grieving the painful loss of their child. Of course, they're not thankful for such an untimely death. How could they be? But because they are in Christ, and in God's will, they are thankful "*in* everything." This status does not negate the pain, but it recognizes God's purpose in the pain to show off His glory.

Certainly, the early American Pilgrims were aware of this. The stories of their 5:18 spirit in those early days are inspiring. And humbling. One scholar claims, "Pilgrims made seven times more graves than huts. No Americans have been more impoverished than these who, nevertheless, set aside a day of Thanksgiving."[4]

James reminds us of the many trials that will come our way.

> My brethren, count it all joy when you fall into various trials, knowing that the testing of your faith produces patience. But let patience have its perfect work, that you may be perfect and complete, lacking nothing. If any of you lacks wisdom, let him ask of God, who gives to all liberally and without reproach, and it will be given to him. (James 1:2–5)

To be thankful "in" everything is to ultimately recognize the reality of Romans 8:28: "And we know that all things work together for good to those who love God, to those who are the called according to His purpose." He's working out all things for the good of those who love Him.

Matthew Henry said that if you call a man ungrateful, you can call him nothing worse. He gives us a healthy perspective on this with these words in his diary after being robbed by thieves: "Let me be thankful, first, because I was never robbed before; second, because, although they took my purse, they did not take my life; third, because, although they took my all, it was not much; and fourth, because it was I who was robbed, not I who robbed."[5]

Question: How often should we be thankful? Answer: How much has God blessed us? If His mercies are from everlasting to everlasting (Ps. 103:17), then our thanksgiving also has no limit! "In everything" is Paul's finite way of expressing gratitude for infinite and undeserved grace. Even in those tough, dark valleys of life, like my good friend Pastor Sam. He was thankful for a freakish bike wreck. He got back up and felt mostly fine after the accident, except for some internal bleeding.

The bleeding alerted his doctors to a malignant tumor they would never have found until it was too late! He gives thanks that the awkward fall and uncomfortable process brought about a lifesaving result.

Another family we know found unexpected thanksgiving in the husband's construction accident. All the terrible injuries from his fall led the doctors to discover a cancerous mass in his body—unrelated to the accident. Now they're thankful that not only did the doctors discover the growth, but they were able to remove it. Today he's cancer-free, and thankful.

Who isn't thankful when a malignant tumor is removed? We may not enjoy the pain, the process, or the procedure, but we're certainly thankful for the result and . . . thankful to live another day to be able to thank the Lord! In life or death, believers in Christ have everything to gain because of all He has given us. If physical healing is not in His plans, the *ultimate* healing of heaven gives us even greater cause for thanksgiving.

So what does it mean to be thankful in everything? The amount of thankfulness isn't limited to an occasion or an event; it is a lifestyle of grace and gratitude. Many people who have not been declared cancer-free or fully recovered are thankful because of the closeness and intimacy with God they've experienced during their pain.

The late J. I. Packer, no stranger to painful medical conditions, noted,

> God uses chronic pain and weakness, along with other afflictions, as his chisel for sculpting our lives. Felt weakness deepens dependence on Christ for strength each day. The weaker we feel, the harder we lean. And the harder we lean, the stronger we grow spiritually, even

> while our bodies waste away. To live with your "thorn" uncomplainingly—that is, sweet, patient, and free in heart to love and help others, even though every day you feel weak—is true sanctification. It is true healing for the spirit. It is a supreme victory of grace.[6]

Just think of the many people these saints have blessed, who ended up going through the same ordeal. God's Word reminds us why His comfort flows to us: so that it can flow through us in everything.

"Blessed be the God and Father of our Lord Jesus Christ, the Father of mercies and God of all comfort, who comforts us in all our tribulation, that we may be able to comfort those who are in any trouble, with the comfort with which we ourselves are comforted by God" (2 Cor. 1:3–4).

How often am I thankful? Even when it hurts? How can I be a channel of thanksgiving flowing downstream to bless others who are in pain?

The greatest example of giving thanks in all circumstances is the Son of God. He even gave thanks for the meal that celebrated His own execution. No one suffered as Jesus did. And He was the only One who was perfect and innocent of any wrong, much less of deserving the death penalty. Yet He was perfectly thankful His entire life, all the way to the cross.

As we'll see more in chapter 6, He is our chief grounds for thanksgiving. A wonderful phrase that embodies the entire message of this book and the 5:18 song I've written is "He Gave Everything, So We Give Thanks." Christ's perfect sacrifice is a gift that we cannot replicate, improve upon, or even model with our best attempts at morality. It can *only* be received. And how is it received? By faith, with joy and thanksgiving! "Therefore, having been justified by faith, we have peace with God through our Lord Jesus Christ, through whom also we have access by faith into this grace in which we stand, and rejoice in hope of the glory of God" (Rom. 5:1–2).

Great Suffering, Great Thanksgiving

When Joni Eareckson Tada was a teenager, a near-fatal diving accident left her a quadriplegic. Yet this beautiful Christian speaker, writer, artist, and philanthropist recently celebrated fifty-plus years of ministry from her rolling pulpit. How did she persevere through all the trials, hardships, pain, and disappointment? She was thankful!

Joni once told me how in her earlier years she went to several faith healers but remained paralyzed. Some well-meaning people piously told her, "You don't have enough faith to be healed." Thank God, Joni didn't allow such a discouraging untruth to ultimately deter her from receiving His greater blessing. She says, "My weakness, that is, my quadriplegia, is my greatest asset because it forces me into the arms of Christ every single morning when I get up."[7]

This woman, who is unable to get down on her knees to pray, has been used mightily by God to bring all kinds of souls from all over the world to their knees. How beautiful that today, because of Joni's grateful heart, someone on the other side of the globe will receive a wheelchair and a gospel presentation. Joni's bold and thanksgiving-filled witness has pointed thousands worldwide to faith in Christ. How many people across the globe are today giving thanks "in everything" because of Joni's vibrant witness—even in her great trials?

How is it that many of those who have been through some of the worst forms of suffering, trauma, trouble, and struggle are some of the most grateful people? I saw this firsthand in 2009 when I ministered among many young genocide victims in the Darfur region of Sudan. These people had nothing and most had lost everything, including family. Yet the hearts of these dear Sudanese Christians were full of gratitude for the water, the food, and the emergency kits we delivered, especially the Bibles and spiritual resources. We need to lean into Romans 8:28, which reminds us: "And we know that all things work together for good to those who love God, to those who are the called according to His purpose." This is not just a "sermonette" for "Christianettes," or simply yet another spiritual anecdote. This thanksgiving verse recognizes that in the crucible of suffering, *all* things, not *some* things, work together for the good of those who love God and are called according to His purpose. Aren't you grateful He's working it all out? There's always a greater purpose in the plan of God.

I recently heard Gary Chapman recount the evening he and Karolyn were sitting on the couch, opening a box of his books that had been translated into other languages. Starting to weep, Karolyn said, "Gary, had we been accepted by the mission board, these books may never have been written and translated into all these languages to impact millions of people."

Then tears filled Dr. Chapman's eyes as well. The tears that flowed from their eyes weren't tears of regret, sorrow, or sadness. They were tears of joy—and thanksgiving.[8]

What a remarkable testimony of the first two profound words of the amount in 1 Thessalonians 5:18—in EVERYTHING:

- God gives us everything to be thankful for.
- God is everything we need.
- God works everything out for His good.

Everything means every time, anytime, and just in time; because God is good . . . *all the time*! As the psalmist exclaimed:

> But we will bless the LORD
> From this time forth and for evermore.
> Praise the LORD! (Ps. 115:18)

Discussion Questions for Chapter 3

1. Why should I be thankful, even when I don't feel like it?
2. Where does an "attitude of gratitude" come from?
3. In what difficult circumstances am I thankful?
4. How has God used trials in my life to bless others?

Living Thanks . . . Write It Down

5. What has this chapter inspired me to record in my gratitude journal?
6. To whom can I send a quick thank-you text?
7. Whom can I thank for being a faithful source of encouragement?

"Gratitude is an offering precious in the sight of God, and it is one that the poorest of us can make and be not poorer but richer for having made it."

A. W. Tozer[1]

CHAPTER 4

The Action—"Give Thanks"

To the end that my glory may sing praise to
You and not be silent.
O LORD my God, I will give thanks to You forever.

PSALM 30:12

We all know that talk is cheap and action is everything. Let's consider the simple word *give.* It's one of the most powerful four-letter words in the Bible. Yes, we've probably been taught that the best way to spell the word *"love"* is "t-i-m-e." But before we can even do this, love must first be spelled "g-i-v-e"! For love can't be expressed by time apart from the action of sacrificial giving.

We also find this good word as the main verb in another famous verse we all know, but we tend to say it way too fast. John 3:16 extols the ultimate gift and giver: "For God so loved the world that He. . . "

The next four-letter word changed history and changed my life! "For God so loved the world that He *gave*." He is a giving God. First Thessalonians 5:18 says, "In everything, *give*."

Who gave first? God! By contrast, we are takers by nature. Thank God that He is, by nature, a giving God. God is love. "Beloved, let us love one another, for love is of God; and everyone who loves is born of God and knows God. He who does not love does not know God, for God is love" (1 John 4:7–8). God, in love, sacrificially gave.

What kind of shape were we in when God gave? To what kind of creatures did He give? He gave to those who had nothing to give back but our sin and failure. As sinners, all we could give to Him was our rebellion. According to Scripture, we were pursuing Him about as much as a bank robber is chasing a cop. We were, in fact, running the other way—straight toward hell. Romans 3:10–11 and 23 speak directly about the kind of people for whom God gave His Son:

> "There is none righteous, no, not one;
> There is none who understands;
> There is none who seeks after God." . . .
> "For all have sinned and fall short of the glory of God."

In our sinful, fallen condition, sinful humans don't want God, God's will, or even God's gifts. Romans 5:8-10 states:

> But God demonstrates His own love towards us, in that while we were still sinners, Christ died for us. Much more then, having now been justified by His blood, we shall be saved from wrath through

> Him. For if when we were enemies we were reconciled to God through the death of His Son, much more, having been reconciled, we shall be saved by His life.

While we were his enemies, he died for us!

Yet in grace, He stooped down and "gave His only begotten Son, that whoever believes in Him should not perish but have everlasting life" (John 3:16). God acted and gave. We react and *give thanks*. Therefore, the amount—in everything—is followed by the action—to give thanks. This is giving on display. We see it in the story of Jesus and the ten lepers. Ten were healed, but only one of them intentionally returned to give thanks. That one was, of all things, a Samaritan—a sworn enemy of the Jews, considered an outcast and unclean.

Here's the account of the ten lepers from Luke 17:11–19.

> Now it happened as He went to Jerusalem that He passed through the midst of Samaria and Galilee. Then as He entered a certain village, there met Him ten men who were lepers, who stood afar off. And they lifted up their voices and said, "Jesus, Master, have mercy on us!"
>
> So when He saw them, He said to them, "Go, show yourselves to the priests." And so it was that as they went, they were cleansed.
>
> And one of them, when he saw that he was healed, returned, and with a loud voice glorified God, and fell down on his face at His feet, giving Him thanks. And he was a Samaritan.
>
> So Jesus answered and said, "Were there not ten cleansed? But where are the nine? Were there not any found who returned to give glory

to God except this foreigner?" And He said to him, "Arise, go your way. Your faith has made you well."

Look at the four things this Samaritan did.

- First, he "returned"—showing intentional action. He didn't fall in with the ungrateful crowd.
- Second, "with a loud voice [he] glorified God." What was in his heart found clear expression from his mouth. Simply saying the words "thank you" can make a huge difference. His "loud" thank-you was certainly heard—to the glory of God (Col. 3:23).
- Third, he "fell on his face." Genuine humility marks the heart of thanksgiving and can often be communicated nonverbally in our posture of thanks.
- Finally, he gave thanks. Thankful people can't hide it. When you've been graciously touched by the Master, thanksgiving just spills out everywhere and in everything. The word *give* comes from the Greek root word *charis*, from which we get the word *grace*.

Idolatrous Ingratitude

Just as giving thanks is an act of faith, its opposite—being ungrateful—is unbelief in action. The grumbling nation of Israel's rebellion was fueled by their ingratitude. Lack of thanks was on Paul's tragic list describing our depraved state in Romans 1:21: "Because, although they knew God, they did not glorify Him as God, nor were thankful, but became futile in their thoughts, and their foolish hearts were darkened."

You can trace almost every crime to a lack of thanksgiving! The violation of all Ten Commandments (see Ex. 20), from "no other gods" to "you shall not covet," stems from an unthankful heart that lives for itself and not its maker. Bitterness, a critical spirit, discontent, lust, and all forms of selfishness flow from and find their expression in unthankfulness. Rather than resting in gratitude for who He is, and all He has provided, we roam aimlessly, construct false idols of the heart, steal from others, and think that all of this will satisfy us.

John Calvin aptly noted that "man's nature is a perpetual factory of idols."[2] This sinful nature tends to find rest, hope, and satisfaction in anything or anyone *other than* the Lord. Thus, ingratitude will always follow (or even lead to) idolatry.

Ingratitude elevates my will above God's and my priorities above His. Why? Because at the root of ingratitude is thinking you didn't get from God or others what you deserve, so you have the right to grab it anyway you can! Ultimately it leads down a dark path, sometimes when we least expect it. Consider seemingly harmless idle talk and coarse jesting. Note the remarkable contrast Paul makes when he says we may engage in "neither filthiness, nor foolish talking, nor coarse jesting, which are not fitting, but rather giving of thanks" (Eph. 5:4). When you find yourself embroiled in a mess of idle, pointless talk, start giving thanks to God for His blessings. As Woodrow Kroll has stated so well, "Concentrate on counting your blessings and you'll have little time to count anything else."[3]

When you do, watch the entire mood change! God gave us our vocal cords, not to gripe, complain, curse, or groan about worthless things. He gave us a voice so we can give Him thanks. The last words in the longest book in the Bible say it best: "Let everything that has breath praise the Lord. Praise the Lord!" (Ps. 150:6).

Unthankfulness even makes another of Paul's rosters of mankind's depravity during the last days. He states in 2 Timothy 3:2, "For men will be lovers of themselves, lovers of money, boasters, proud, blasphemers, disobedient to parents, unthankful, unholy."

In *King Lear*, Shakespeare writes, "How sharper than a serpent's tooth it is to have a thankless child."[4] Pastor Robert Green Lee wisely stated,

> The thief may have in him streaks of honesty, the dead beat spots of honor, the liar occasional impulses to tell the truth, the libertine, some desires to be pure. But there is nothing redemptive in the ingrate. Trust the ungrateful soul with money, he will steal it; with honor, he will betray it; with virtue, he will violate it; With a blood-bequeathed legacy, he will reduce it in quality and quantity. Trust the ingrate with love—and with hellish alchemy, he will transmute it into lust. Trust the ingrate with your good name—he will besmirch it. Ingratitude is . . . a most common disease of humanity. Many fail more often in gratitude than in any other Christian graces.[5]

We can certainly trust Jesus Christ, who personified perfect gratitude. In preparing for His great sacrifice, on the night He was betrayed, Jesus Himself gave thanks when He instituted the "thanksgiving feast" of the new covenant. The word for the Lord's Supper, *eucharist*, comes from the Greek word for giving thanks (more on this in chapter 5).

Consider the significance of this moment mere hours before Good Friday. Jesus was thanking God for the breaking of His own body and the spilling of His own blood. Who better to model giving thanks "in everything" than the one who gave everything? Every sacrifice offered in the Old Testament was somehow connected to giving thanks. And all those slain lambs pointed to the Lamb of God who gave His life to take away the sins of the world (John 1:29).

In the same way, the Greek word translated as "forgive," χαρίζομαι, literally means to "give grace."[6] So "thanks-giving" involves an active, volitional movement on the part of the thankful one. The word *give* connects to every other sacrificial instance of "giving/give/gift" in the Bible. To "give thanks" is a responsive "give back"—not necessarily of material value, but of the heart. Ten lepers were given a complete healing—only one gave thanks.

What has God given? He gave us everything in Christ. How can we repay or improve on what Jesus has done for us? We can give back thanks to Him with our lives and our lips (John 3:16; 2 Cor. 9:15; Heb. 13:15; Rom. 6:17).

Happy Thanks-Praising

Because giving praise and giving thanks are so connected, we often use them interchangeably—and that's not such a bad thing. This passage helps illustrate:

> In thanksgiving we list God's benefits, in praise God is the benefit. Thanksgiving is like a child opening a gift from a parent, a new doll or a baseball mitt, and throwing her arms around her mom and dad and saying, "Thank you, thank you! It's just what I wanted. It's

> wonderful!" Praise is what happens when that child can pause and look up from the gift into her folks' eyes and say, "You are wonderful." There is, in prayer and worship, a kind of ascendancy that moves from thanks to praise to wonder to awe and silence—and then back again to thanks to praise to wonder to awe to silence.[7]

The beauty of thanksgiving and thanks-praising is the essential connection of who God is with what He does. Without recognizing the beauty of the infinite character of our triune God, there can be *no* thanksgiving. God's heart is for us to seek after His person above His provision. We praise Him as the Giver and we thank Him for His gifts. Our greatest desire should be for the Giver rather than the gift. Yet how often do we get this backwards? We tend to enjoy His "presents," but it is in His "presence" where we find "fullness of joy" and "pleasures forevermore" (Ps. 16:11).

Matthew 6:33, my mother's favorite verse, is a great reminder that all He provides will be "added to us" when we seek Him and His kingdom first. We see this both in creation and redemption. We sing this in the great doxology, "Praise God from whom all blessings flow, praise Him all creatures here below. Praise Him above ye heavenly host. Praise Father, Son and Holy Ghost."

We praise God for who He is, and we thank God for what He has done.

But it's also okay to do the reverse. As long as the heart is right, the mouth will follow. With Isaac Watts, may we ask the Lord to "tune my heart to sing thy grace."[8] Most importantly, we thank Him for what He has done for us in Christ, to redeem us and make us His own.

Let us never forget that our greatest blessings are spiritual, eternal, and invisible (2 Cor. 4:18)! He's given us His priceless treasure in our earthen vessels (v. 7). Yes! He is our God who heals the body, but our bodies on this earth won't last forever—until we get resurrection bodies (2 Cor. 5:1–5). The spiritual benefits and blessings of God will carry into eternity. They will never end and in fact will become sweeter and sweeter.

In salvation, we praise God's merciful, gracious, loving, slow-to-anger, faithful, and just character. As a result, we thank God for all the benefits—forgiveness of sin, unfailing love, new life, new identity—and the hope of heaven—justification, sanctification, glorification.

What's Your Sign?

When we express our gratitude to God, He often gives us better good things for which we can be thankful.

One day at my favorite local Christian bookstore, I noticed a bunch of merchandise with the words "Thank You, Jesus" on them. I asked the owner about all of these products and how they sold. He told me they sold thousands of the signs, magnets, and other items with this message on them.

How is my life one big "Thank You, Jesus" sign? When people see me, do they see a thankful person? Why is thanksgiving an *action*? Why does the psalmist say, "I will bless the Lord at all times" (Ps. 34:1)? Why are we to "enter into His gates with thanksgiving" (Ps. 100:4)? It's simple. The answer is in verse 3 of this famous thanksgiving psalm, also known as the "Old 100."

Know that the LORD, He is God;
It is He who has made us, and not we ourselves;
We are His people and the sheep of His pasture.

The psalmist goes on in verse 5 to state three unalterable, eternal facts that give us great cause for praise and thanksgiving:

1. The LORD is good,
2. His mercy is everlasting, and
3. His truth endures.

Just think of how encouraged you are when a friend calls just to say "thank you." The act of simply picking up the phone to give thanks deepens the joy for both you and the other person. When it comes to our relationship with God, thanksgiving is a supremely important response of faith! By faith we receive His amazing gift to us; by faith we give thanks to Him.

So ask yourself: What action am I taking to give thanks? What do I do? Why not start with a simple "thank you"? Start right there. Like the merchandise in the bookstore—"Thank You, Jesus." Say that out loud today. The healed leper said it real loud. He realized the simple truth that we have received infinitely more than we've ever given.

Dietrich Bonhoeffer said it this way: "In ordinary life we hardly realize that we receive a great deal more than we give, and that it is only with gratitude that life becomes rich."[9] May the words "Thank You, Jesus!" be much on our thankful lips.

Discussion Questions for Chapter 4

1. Who has modeled thankfulness for me?
2. What has God given to me?
3. How intentional am I about giving thanks?
4. When's the last time I wrote a thank-you note by hand?

Living Thanks . . . Write It Down

5. What has this chapter inspired me to record in my gratitude journal?
6. Today, whom can I thank in person?
7. To whom can I write a thank-you note for giving me that first opportunity in a job, ministry, or new career?

"God is in control, and therefore in everything I can give thanks—not because of the situation but because of the One who directs and rules over it."

Kay Arthur[1]

CHAPTER 5

The Aim—"This Is the Will of God"

"Therefore do not be unwise, but understand what the will of the Lord is."

EPHESIANS 5:17

Decades ago, in a small hotel room in Boston, my dad, my mom, and my Uncle Ed got on their knees to seek God's will about buying "the best" station to spread His Word. The decision to move forward could put everything they had done in Christian radio at great risk. The Lord answered their prayer and provided a wonderful station, WEZE, that is still touching souls today.

I thank God that my parents were deeply committed to living in His will. They made the will of God the standard for all of our family decisions. In fact, if it were not for their influence in this area, I would not be writing this book encouraging you in the same heavenly direction.

From the time we were tiny children, Mom and Dad consistently prayed for our salvation, our future spouses, college decisions, and careers. It took me many years before I understood the importance of God's will in everything.

I'll never forget, during my freshman year in college, hearing a well-known pastor deliver a powerful message in chapel. It was about finding God's will. The message couldn't have come at a better time. I was looking for direction, struggling with my ultimate purpose, and emotionally twisted like a pretzel. Life was coming at me fast as I was trying to figure out God's will.

The speaker's text was Romans 12:1–2:

> I beseech you therefore, brethren, by the mercies of God, that you present your bodies a living sacrifice, holy, acceptable to God, which is your reasonable service. And do not be conformed to this world, but be transformed by the renewing of your mind, that you may prove what is that good and acceptable and perfect will of God.

His main point: "Stop looking for God's will." It sent shock waves across the packed auditorium. At this point, we were all thinking, *Wait a second! Isn't this why we came to a solid Christian liberal arts university? Wasn't this the most important thing in life?*

The speaker's next words made an indelible imprint on my life. He said, "Seek God, and 'His will' will find you!" Here's the point: God's Word working in you, by the power of the Holy Spirit, brings you face-to-face with His will. As the psalmist says in Psalm 37:4, "Delight yourself also in the LORD, And He shall give you the desires of your heart."

Or as Jesus said in John 15:7, "If you abide in Me, and My words abide in you, you will ask what you desire, and it shall be done for you."

So, what is God's will? *God's will is simply what God wants.* Back to the speaker's point: To know what God wants, you must first come to know God. Then remember that He reveals His will in His Word. God's Word expresses God's will to us. Want to know His will? Open your Bible. Ask Him to show you. As I've told my basketball guys, "Every time you open the Word of God, you're getting a text directly from God." Remember, like us, with God's words goes God's breathe. To read Scripture is to sit under the spigot of the Holy Spirit. "All Scripture is given by inspiration of God, and is profitable for doctrine, for reproof, for correction, for instruction in righteousness." (2 Tim 3:16)

Knowing Him is knowing His will. Living in His will is living in fellowship with the Father, through the Son, and by the power of the Holy Spirit.

There's no greater aim, purpose, or destiny than the perfect will of God. God's will is central to all of life. According to the *Westminster Shorter Catechism*, the chief end of man is "to glorify God and enjoy Him forever." Here are the first two questions. Note their simple yet profound answers with the rich accompanying Scriptures.[2]

Q. 1. What is the chief end of man?

A. Man's chief end is to glorify God, and to enjoy him for ever.

Glorify God: Ps. 86:9; Isa. 60:21; Rom. 11:36; 1 Cor. 6:20; 10:31; Rev. 4:11

Enjoy Him Forever: Ps. 16:5–11; 144:15; Isa. 12:2; Luke 2:10; Phil. 4:4; Rev. 21:3–4

Q. 2. What rule hath God given to direct us in how we may glorify and enjoy him?

A. The Word of God, which is contained in the Scriptures of the Old and New Testaments, is the only rule to direct us in how we may glorify and enjoy him.

Word of God: Matt. 19:4–5 with Gen. 2:24; Luke 24:27, 44; 1 Cor. 2:13; 14:37; 2 Peter 1:20–21; 3:2, 15–16

Only Rule: Deut. 4:2; Ps. 19:7–11; Isa. 8:20; John 15:11; 20:30–31; Acts 17:11; 2 Tim. 3:15–17; 1 John 1:4

He is Creator God and He created us in His image and for His pleasure. His will is to be the burning desire of every believer. The will of God is revealed in the Word of God. There is no safer place to be than in the center of God's will. To be in God's will means to be in his presence - what better place to be than in his presence, wherever that place on earth might be. There's no more dangerous place in the world than being outside His will. If I'm washing toilets at the gas station in the slums and that's God's will, that's the best place I could ever be. Or, if I'm pulling down seven figures, but outside of God's will, that's the worst, most dangerous place I could ever be! As Nancy DeMoss Wolgemuth so wisely said,

> An evidence that our will has been broken is that we begin to thank God for that which once seemed so bitter, knowing that His will is good and that, in His time and in His way, He is able to make the most bitter waters sweet.[3]

God's will is so simple, yet we make it so complicated. The result of knowing God is knowing His will. And His will always leads to thanksgiving. If it's God's will to give thanks in *everything*, then we will be ever thankful every moment we abide in God's will. What a simple way to tell if someone is walking in the will of God—he or she will be full of thanks to God! God's will is his love in action - what better reason to give thanks than seeing God work everything in our lives according to his loving purpose for us, i.e., to good.

Paul closes out Romans 12:2 with a blessed description of God's will as "what is good and acceptable and perfect."

The will of God isn't just here on earth, but it takes us all the way into glory. But in the meantime, it brings His glory down to earth. Jesus, in the Lord's Prayer, says, "Your will be done on earth as it is in heaven" (Luke 11:2b). To be thankful is to be heavenly minded while living on earth.

Guess what we'll be doing forever in heaven? Read Revelation 4:10–11, 7:9–17, 19:1–10, and many other passages. We'll be giving thanks *forever*. Heaven is simply the consummation and continuation of the will of God and thanksgiving to the Lamb of God. John contrasted the fading nature of the world with the forever glory of His will: "And the world is passing away, and the lust of it; but he who does the will of God abides forever" (1 John 2:17).

The tragic opposite of abiding in God's glorious will is abiding in the lake of fire. Hell is the eternal epitome of a lack of thanksgiving and the terror of endless ingratitude. Conversely, in heaven, we'll live with Jesus in a place full of perfect thanksgiving. Our ultimate aim of God's will carries us all the way to heaven and into eternity.

We saw this approach to gratitude in the life of my dad. As a young father, he daily prayed with my three sisters and me to seek God's will. He and Mom passionately prayed with us at family devotions that we would always "put the Lord first" in our lives. The older Dad got, the more these prayers intensified. He also became more thankful—even in his health struggles. His gratefulness became a blessing to us all. He constantly gave thanks in prayer and conversation.

Rarely would we end a family gathering without a prayer session or simply a brief word of thanks to the Lord. Even in family disputes, he would often remark, "How wonderful that we're so blessed to have these problems to argue about!" When Dad stepped into heaven, not only did his faith become sight, but his *thanks* became sight.

In the book of Revelation, the apostle John gives us a clearer glimpse of our eternal, thankful state:

> After these things I looked, and behold, a great multitude which no one could number, of all nations, tribes, peoples, and tongues, standing before the throne and before the Lamb, clothed with white robes, with palm branches in their hands, and crying out with a loud voice, saying, "Salvation belongs to our God who sits on the throne, and to the Lamb!" (Rev. 7:9–10; see also Rev. 19:1–10)

Heaven is a place of unencumbered, unrestrained thanksgiving to God for all of eternity. Hell is the tragic opposite. Thanksgiving is the language of heaven. Grumbling is the language of hell.

Heaven resounds with thanksgiving and the highest expression of God's perfect will. All those redeemed by the blood of the Lamb will be glorified. There will be no tears, pain, separation, sin, or shame. There will be an infinitely perpetual and thoroughly gratifying state of thanksgiving.

Heaven will be eternal thanksgiving (Rev. 4:9; 7:11–12; 11:16–17). Thanksgiving is always aligned with His perfect will. While thanksgiving is the language of Heaven, grumbling is the language of Hell.

Do you want to know what hell is? Not only is it full of weeping, gnashing of teeth, shame, and regret, but it's completely devoid of gratitude. How frightening. There are so many biblical examples of the devastation of a lack of thanksgiving. We already mentioned the "grumbling" children of Israel in the wilderness (Ex. 16:12; Num. 11:1–2). There's also the tragic state of the ungodly in Romans 1:21. Fundamentally, hell is an eternal rejection of God's perfect will. And its flames burn darkly in the ultimate, tragic antithesis of thanksgiving.

Ephesians 5:20 celebrates the all-important aim of our being: "Giving thanks always for all things to God the Father in the name of our Lord Jesus Christ." It's the thankful response to walking in God's will. It's a chorus, according to 5:19, of "speaking to one another in psalms and hymns and spiritual songs, singing and making melody in your heart to the Lord." It flows out of the command in Ephesians 5:18, "Do not be drunk with wine, in which is dissipation; but be filled with the Spirit."

But even before Paul rallies his readers (including you and me) to this Spirit-filled hallelujah chorus, he goes straight to the business of God's will. Ephesians 5:17 says, "Therefore do not be unwise, but understand what the will of the Lord is." A Spirit-filled life is a life aligned with God's will. It's a life guided by God's wisdom, full of the Holy Spirit, and abounding in thanksgiving. And, yes, there will be singing!

Several years ago, we were heartbroken to learn that one of our favorite college Bible professors was diagnosed with terminal cancer. To my surprise, he came on my national radio show and publicly thanked God for his cancer. Dr. C. W. Smith couldn't have been more excited and thankful about the ultimate healing of heaven that soon awaited him. Listeners even called in to challenge him and talk him out of his spirit of thanksgiving. He had always taught us in the classroom about pursuing and delighting in the will of God. In fact, I took a class on the book of Romans from him. Decades later, when the going got rough, we witnessed his syllabus become a "real-abus," as he beautifully displayed living in God's will—even in the face of death. I'll never forget his legacy and impact.

Let's go back to that hotel room prayer meeting in Boston. Not only did God's will prevail in the blessing of a radio station, but decades later, thanksgiving flooded a corporate suite in a New York high-rise. Dad, Uncle Ed, and I were meeting with a high-level executive. As we were getting acquainted, this executive unexpectedly shared how his wife came to faith in Christ listening to WEZE driving in Boston. Through her witness, he, too, followed Jesus and has faithfully served the Lord for years.

Thank God for using my folks, Dr. Smith, Joni Eareckson Tada, and so many other dear saints—past and present—as powerful testaments of His sustaining grace to those whose aim is His perfect will. The testimony of thanksgiving in the face of setbacks, difficulties, and even deadly circumstances can only come from someone who has experienced the transforming power of the gospel of Jesus Christ. I can only pray that God will give me the same thankful heart in the face of such trials.

Let us ever remember: His will is perfect. His grace is sufficient. How thankful are we for the perfect will of God?

Discussion Questions for Chapter 5

1. Why is knowing God essential to knowing God's will?
2. How does being thankful remind me who's really in control?
3. When in my life have I been thankful for God's will working all things together for the good?
4. How do my loved ones see my thankfulness for God's perfect plan in my life?

Living Thanks . . . Write It Down

5. What has this chapter inspired me to record in my gratitude journal?
6. Whom can I honor today with a nice thank-you message?
7. To whom can I write a thank-you note for coaching, mentoring, or discipling me in the formative years of my life?

"Gratitude is the ability to experience life as a gift. It liberates us from the prison of self-preoccupation."

John Ortberg[1]

CHAPTER 6

The Access—"In Christ Jesus"

For you know the grace of our Lord Jesus Christ, that though He was rich, yet for your sakes He became poor, that you through His poverty might become rich.

2 Corinthians 8:9

So, where does thanksgiving come from? Perhaps a better question is, *Who* does thanksgiving come from? The answer: Jesus Christ. He is the personification and the incarnation of God's will on earth. Everything God willed *for* us, Jesus Christ delivered *to* us when He came *to save* us. He is "the way" (John 14:6). He is the "one mediator" between God and man (1 Tim. 2:15). The Father sent the Son to bring us to Him, to reconcile us to God, to make us new (2 Cor. 5:17–21).

And our reasons for thanksgiving keep getting better. Those who put their full trust in Him have been granted full access to the Father by Him. Take a moment and contemplate the gravity of these three profound words: "In Christ Jesus." Jesus Christ *is* the access to *everything* God willed for us. "For God so loved the world, He gave His only Son." Paul uses the words "in Christ" or "in Him" over 143 times in his epistles.

So, you have the amount, "in everything." You have the action, "give thanks." You have the aim, "God's will." But how do we get there? We must have access, and the only access is "in Christ Jesus." He is the bridge to life. Without Him, we are lost.

Consider the many ways the gospel of John presents Jesus—they are revealed in the great "I Am" statements. He is the living Word (John 1:14). He is the living water (John 4:14; 7:37). He is the living bread (John 6:35). He is the light of the world (John 8:12). He is the door to life (John 10:7). He is the good shepherd (John 10:11). He is the resurrection and the life (John 11:25). He is the life-giving vine (John 15:1). He is the way, the truth, the life; no one comes to the Father except through Him (John 14:6).

The way to God is not a plan, a bunch of principles, prohibitions, processes, or a pledge. It's simply found in a *person*. Jesus Christ is the only way we can give thanks to God. This is because God gave Jesus as the only way to save us. His-story is the scarlet thread of redemption woven throughout all of Scripture—from Genesis to Revelation.

We can only be reconciled to God and become children of God through Christ. No Jesus, no way. No Jesus, no peace. No Jesus, no access. But . . . know Jesus . . . know the way; know Jesus . . . know peace; know Jesus . . . know access. He *is* the way. He *paved* the way. And He *paid* the way—in His own blood. Paul reminds us of the abounding thanksgiving that comes from being rooted and built up in Christ: "As you therefore have received Christ Jesus the Lord, so walk in Him, rooted and built up in Him and established in the faith, as you have been taught, abounding in it with thanksgiving" (Col. 2:6–7).

How does Jesus personify the five A's of 5:18? This simple chart demonstrates this.

He controls the **amount.**
"In everything" . . . Jesus is in control of everything, and He is our everything. (Col. 1:16, 17; 2:9, 10)

He compels the **action.**
"Give thanks" . . . Jesus took action "while we were yet sinners" and gave His life so we could have life and give thanks. (1 John 3:16)

He completes the **aim.**
"This is God's will" . . . Jesus completely fulfilled God's will and brings us into alignment with the will of God. (Gal. 1:4)

He connects the **access.**
"In Christ Jesus" . . . We are in Him and covered by Him, and we come to the Father through Him. (John 14:6; 1 Tim. 2:5))

He conveys the **application.**
"Concerning you" . . . In Christ, we have a new life, righteousness, and meaning applied to us. (2 Peter 1:3)

Happy Thanks-Feasting!

Did you know that in every Bible feast we celebrate Jesus Christ? In fact, He made every Bible feast and festival possible. He is the hero of both the old and new covenant feasts. Paul extols Christ's sufficiency in his words to the church at Colossae, when the feasts were distracting rather than displaying Jesus: "So let no one judge you in food or in drink, or regarding a festival or a new moon or sabbaths, which are a shadow of things to come, but the substance is of Christ" (Col. 2:16–17).

As mentioned in chapter 2, Jesus fulfilled the old covenant Passover feast. He "gave thanks" when He instituted the first New Testament thanksgiving feast:

> For I received from the Lord that which I also delivered to you: that the Lord Jesus on the same night in which He was betrayed took bread; and when He had given thanks, He broke it and said, "Take, eat; this is My body which is broken for you; do this in remembrance of Me." (1 Cor. 11:23–24)

You'll recall from chapter 4 that the Greek word for "give thanks" is *Eucharistio* or *eucharisteō.*

This word is actually a combination of several things in the ancient Greek language. Eu is a prefix meaning "good," so a eulogy is a speaking of the good of a dead person and euthanasia is a good death. Charis means "grace" or "favor," so eucharisteo means something like "thanksgiving as giving favor to others well." But charis is closely related to the Greek word chara, which literally means joy.[2] What a power-packed word!

But why would Jesus, the Giver of all life, need to give thanks?

Let's go back in time. Our New Testament Lord's Supper—also called Communion—has its roots in the Passover feast. This originated back before the exodus of the children of Israel from Egypt.

What happened when they celebrated the first Passover? Did you know that it was also a thanksgiving feast? They were deeply grateful that death didn't enter their homes. The death angel did not look inside at the families huddled around their tables to see if they were worthy or not. Rather, he looked at the blood on the door mantel and "passed over," not killing the firstborn (Ex. 11). The people received mercy. This Passover feast was an annual celebration of thanksgiving. The angel of death passed over them so they could go pass over from slavery to freedom in the promised land.

Since then, every time a Jewish family gathers at Passover, they partake of an unblemished lamb and unleavened bread. In essence, the members are saying, "Thank You, God, for delivering us from four hundred years of slavery in Egypt."

The feasts of the Bible are all in some way connected to giving thanks.[3] Some are agricultural in origin, marking the different stages of the harvest season. The people celebrated the abundant provision of God. Others, such as the Passover, were intended to give thanks to God for His glorious deliverance. In the Feast of Tabernacles, the people gave thanks for God's faithful provision of food and water on their long sojourn in the wilderness. Meals were shared. Worship and fellowship were enjoyed. To this day, the Jewish people observe many feasts, and the driving force of them all is thanksgiving.

Fast-forward to the Passover Lamb, Jesus Christ. "The next day John saw Jesus coming toward him, and said, 'Behold! The Lamb of God who takes away the sin of the world!'" (John 1:29). When He took the bread, He broke it and gave thanks (Luke 22:19). That's why we call it the Eucharist, the Lord's Supper, or Holy Communion. Eucharist in English is a translation of the Greek verb εὐχαριστέω ("to give thanks") that occurs in the words of institution given by Jesus. A rich word, εὐχαριστέω communicates a vital and fundamental truth in the Lord's Supper.

Every time you observe the New Testament Passover and take Communion at your church, you're enjoying a thanksgiving feast. You are giving thanks in your heart, your soul, and your mind for the great things He has done. This giving of thanks even involves your taste buds. You partake and digest the elements to truly "taste and see that the Lord is good" (Ps. 34:8). His body was broken for us, and His precious blood was spilled for us that we may be redeemed, made whole, and be full of thanks.

The feast recognizes that none of us is worthy. Only His body and blood are. That's why the only two menu items are the bread and wine. Only His broken body and spilled blood could satisfy the wrath of the Father on our behalf. Through Jesus' worthy sacrifice, He makes *us* worthy. We are made sons and daughters of the Most High! As the blood on the wooden door mantels covered the Hebrews, so the blood on the wooden cross covers the believer in mercy and grace.

Jesus Christ has given; we are forgiven. Therefore, we give thanks! David Jeremiah describes the rich symbolism in the feast of Passover from Exodus 12:6–14:

> God commanded the Hebrew people to keep the feast of Passover as an everlasting ordinance, and Jewish people still do. They commemorate this night when God miraculously protected their ancestors from the plague of death; most, however, do not understand that the Passover ultimately points to the redemption brought by Christ. The roasted flesh of the lamb was to be accompanied with bitter herbs, reminding the children of Israel of their bitter bondage in Egypt. Their haste in eating, combined with their clothing, represented their readiness to travel. So did the unleavened bread.[4]

The reason for commanding the people to make unleavened bread is given in Exodus 12:34–39. The first Passover meal was prepared with urgency because the people had no idea when they were to leave. Properly prepared, raised bread is a time-consuming task. Unleavened bread could be made much more quickly.

The Passover lamb itself prefigured Jesus (John 1:29, 36; 1 Cor. 5:7)—the perfect and sinless Lamb of God (2 Cor. 5:21; 1 Peter 2:21–22; 1 John 3:5). The sacrificial blood, painted on the doorframes of the houses, not only saved the Hebrew people in Egypt from death, it pointed to the shed blood of Jesus and His defeat over eternal death (Rom. 6:9).[5]

Thanksgiving places the rightful emphasis on what Jesus has done for lost sinners. The gospel is not about what we've done for Him, what we're doing for Him, or what we will try to do for Him. It's *all* about what He has done for us in His perfect life, death, and resurrection. He was perfectly on task. Even in His first recorded words as a lad: "Why did you seek Me? Did you not know that I must be about My Father's business?" (Luke 2:49).

He prayed it in His great High Priestly Prayer, saying, "I have glorified You on the earth. I have finished the work which You have given Me to do" (John 17:4). He proclaimed it in His great victory cry from the cross, summarized in those three words in English and one word in the Greek: *tetelestai*, "It is finished!" (John 19:30).

Jesus perfectly fulfilled the will of God. Where the first Adam failed, the second Adam succeeded to redeem the fallen sons of Adam. *He* did it; *He* gave! Now *we* give thanks. He made a way when there was *no* way. He made a way when we were *far* away and when we ran the other way. He brought peace to our restless, unthankful hearts. This is the unconditional love of God poured out.

> In this the love of God was manifested toward us, that God has sent His only begotten Son into the world, that we might live through Him. In this is love, not that we loved God, but that He loved us and sent His Son to be the propitiation for our sins. (1 John 4:9–10)

What other belief has its royal deity coming to die for undeserving sinners, and dying in the worst way possible? As skeptical historian Tom Holland marveled in his bestseller *Dominion: How the Christian Revolution Remade the World*:

> To be a Christian is to believe that God became man and suffered a death as terrible as any mortal has ever suffered. This is why the cross, that ancient implement of torture, remains what it has always been:

> the fitting symbol of the Christian revolution. It is the audacity of . . . finding in a twisted and defeated corpse the glory of the creator of the universe—that serves to explain, more surely than anything else, the sheer strangeness of Christianity, and of the civilisation to which it gave birth.[6]

Whoever would have conceived of a noble king laying down his life for his own subjects? Yet the blessed hope of every Christian is that Jesus not only defeated death, paying the penalty for our sins, but He triumphantly rose again on the third day to prove that God has forgiven us. This is why the gospel is the driving force of our thanksgiving. Countless religions have been practiced across the world, from the beginning of history up until the present day. But there has been only *one* empty tomb.

The Reformers' approach to the whole Christian life is often summed up in two words, "grace" and "gratitude". If you're not sure where to start, consider the amazing grace of God. Go to the cross. Behold the Lamb of God. Linger there. Gaze into the empty tomb. Allow His grace to heal and wash over you.

Then thank God that the tomb is empty so our life can be full! Thank God for unlimited access in Christ. Give thanks for *all* that He has done for you. Give thanks that He lives inside you!

If you've never believed and rested in His perfect work, then do so today, "For whoever calls on the name of the Lord shall be saved" (Rom. 10:13). If you've been saved, then you need to be baptized to publicly profess and thank Him for saving you!

Believers must regularly feast at His table. Drink from the Psalms. Be thankful. May your gratitude be an attitude of response to His perfect redeeming work and not an "add-itude" trying to add to and improve on His work. "May this gratitude overflow in both how you live and how you love." Enter into His gates with thanksgiving (Ps. 100:4).

> But now in Christ Jesus you who once were far off have been brought near by the blood of Christ. For He Himself is our peace, who has made both one, and has broken down the middle wall of separation. (Eph. 2:13–14)

What else can I do but open my heart, then open my mouth, and say, "Thank You, Jesus"? Sometimes when I want to say thank you, the words won't even come out because my heart is so overwhelmed with joy and gratitude.

You don't have to start there. Instead, start by being thankful for the obvious things, such as the air you breathe, the clothes you wear, the roof over your head, your family. If you have food, shelter, and clothing, you're already wealthier than the majority of the world's population. His grace empowers us to stop worrying *about* everything and be thankful *in* everything. How often do we reflect on all He has blessed us with—specifically? "Bless the LORD, O my soul, and forget not all His benefits" (Ps. 103:2).

Gratitude > Grudges

All of us, at some point, have fallen prey to holding a grudge. Here's a practical, thanks-living practice for dealing with that person you are struggling with and sense that roots of bitterness are starting to take hold

(Heb. 12:14–15).

Take a moment and ask God to show you one or two things you can be thankful for. Perhaps something redemptive they've done in the past? Perhaps some survival lessons learned from the conflict? Everyone bears the image of God and has something that we can thank God for. Maybe a difficult person drove you to a closer relationship with Christ. One of my many adopted younger brothers took the "gratitude greater than grudge" challenge recently. He shared with me how thanksgiving helped him in one of these difficult relationships: "Two things came to mind that really helped me have a heart of forgiveness toward this gentleman that has made life really difficult in the past. First, I'm thankful for his drive and ambition that has taught me to work hard. Second, I'm thankful for the valuable lessons of patience and grace that God has taught me in dealing with such a difficult personality. Gratitude always triumphs over grudges."

Christ has also given us access to a new path of forgiveness. The greatest perspective takes us all the way back to the cross, and to gratefully offer forgiveness just as He forgave you (Eph. 4:32). Thanks-living is "living thanks," even to overcome a difficult grudge.

The next time you're upset with someone, find something redeeming about them to be thankful for and watch the Lord change your heart.

Then thank Him for the big things, like being a child of the Most High God. As J. I. Packer and Carolyn Nystrom write, "Adoption is the highest privilege that the gospel offers: higher even than justification. . . . To be right with God the Judge is a great thing, but to be loved and cared for by God the Father is greater."[7]

Read Ephesians 1:3–14, and thank God for all the immense treasure trove of blessings He's given you in Christ.

> Blessed be the God and Father of our Lord Jesus Christ, who has blessed us with every spiritual blessing in the heavenly places in Christ, just as He chose us in Him before the foundation of the world, that we should be holy and without blame before Him in love, having predestined us to adoption as sons by Jesus Christ to Himself, according to the good pleasure of His will, to the praise of the glory of His grace, by which He made us accepted in the Beloved.
>
> In Him we have redemption through His blood, the forgiveness of sins, according to the riches of His grace which He made to abound toward us in all wisdom and prudence, having made known to us the mystery of His will, according to His good pleasure which He purposed in Himself, that in the dispensation of the fullness of the times He might gather together in one all things in Christ, both which are in heaven and which are on earth—in Him. In Him also we have obtained an inheritance, being predestined according to the purpose of Him who works all things according to the counsel of His will, that we who first trusted in Christ should be to the praise of His glory.
>
> In Him you also trusted, after you heard the word of truth, the gospel of your salvation; in whom also, having believed, you were sealed with the Holy Spirit of promise, who is the guarantee of our inheritance until the redemption of the purchased possession, to the praise of His glory.

We can enter His gates with thanksgiving because He's split the gates of heaven wide open for us! In fact, He *is* the gate to eternal life. And He's also the door into the abundant life.

> I am the door. If anyone enters by Me, he will be saved, and will go in and out and find pasture. The thief does not come except to steal, and to kill, and to destroy. I have come that they may have life, and that they may have it more abundantly. (John 10:9–10).

Here's another wonderful verse that contains the amount, the action, the aim, and the access—all in one place:

> Giving thanks always for all things to God the Father in the name of our Lord Jesus Christ. (Eph. 5:20).

Who is the access? Jesus Christ! What is the application? We are! We'll explore and celebrate the immense wealth we receive in our next chapter as we look at the fifth A of 5:18 . . . the application.

Discussion Questions for Chapter 6

1. From what did Jesus save me?
2. How do we see thanksgiving in the feasts of the Bible?
3. What access am I granted "in Christ Jesus"?
4. Have I believed and received the gift of salvation?

Living Thanks . . . Write It Down

5. What has this chapter inspired me to record in my gratitude journal?
6. To whom today can I send a "thank you" message?
7. Whom can I write a thank-you for first telling me about Jesus?

"Yes, give thanks for 'all things' for, as it has been well said, 'Our disappointments are but His appointments.'"

A. W. Pink[1]

CHAPTER 7

The Application—"Concerning You"

For all things are for your sakes, that grace, having spread through the many, may cause thanksgiving to abound to the glory of God.

2 CORINTHIANS 4:15

Robby Dilmore—also known as the Christian Car Guy—is one of our favorite syndicated hosts for Truth Network. Robby's also one of the most thankful people I know, and he has surely had some "book of Job experiences." I guess we say he has had lots of "on the Job" thanksgiving training.

Dilmore shares the most painful of all the tests God has used to grow him in his faith:

The most painful was a brain abscess that resulted from a staph infection born from a titanium plate that was placed in my skull following a brain biopsy. But one day my brain was swelling, and they needed to do emergency surgery to remove the plate and release the pressure in my skull.

Nothing for me was close to the pain of that day. The medical team members had some sort of problem waiting for an operating room and tried every pain-relieving injection they could, but nothing even made a dent. So they finally shut off the lights in the room and encouraged me to hang on somehow.

That's when God showed up in the form of a nurse named Ramona (my eyes still tear up when I recall it). She just simply said, "Robby, I'm here," and held my hand. I know not how, but I knew then and I know today, it was God who was with me, and, spiritually speaking, it was God holding my hand. What gratitude I experienced for this simple but necessary grace.

Then, after the infection almost took my life, I was stuck in the same hospital room for 30 days, mostly in the dark. I was facing the very real possibility of death as I never really have, before or since. Then one day came the light. An attendant was to wheel me via a tunnel under the street for another MRI. Knowing how long I had been in that room in the dark, he asked if I would like a short sidetrack outside. What joy and gratitude I experienced as I was kindly but briefly wheeled into the light of day.[2]

Robby is living proof that orthodoxy (right doctrine) must lead to orthopraxy (right living), whatever life throws at us. Another way to put it: Theology must be expressed in doxology. We will behave exactly as we believe. The thanksgiving that springs up in a heart changed by Jesus will show up in the life that follows Jesus. It will then speak up, giving thanks to Him in everything.

So, we have the amount, "in everything." We have the action: "give thanks." The aim: "this is God's will." And we have the access of amazing grace "in Christ Jesus." Finally, we have the application: "concerning *you*."

How wonderful that *we* are the undeserving beneficiaries of His amazing gift. Because He acted in giving us His Son, we simply react in giving thanks for His Son. Gratitude flows from us because His redeeming grace flowed to us. We were objects of His wrath, but in Christ we have become objects of His love. We have been adopted and made His beloved sons and daughters. As John 1:12 says, "But as many as received Him, to them He gave the right to become children of God, to those who believe in His name."

Here's a little friendly advice: *Don't ever ask God to give you what you deserve.* If you are crazy enough to request this, you had better run for cover! Thank God He has *not* given us what we deserve. The prophet Jeremiah reminds us in Lamentations 3:22 that "through the Lord's mercies we are not consumed."

What is mercy? Mercy is God withholding His wrath—*not* giving me what I *do* deserve. What is grace? Grace goes a step further. It is God lavishing His love on me—giving me what I *do not* deserve. What a glorious thought! This is what God has done "concerning you."

Through His poverty, we have become wealthy beyond measure. We are the rich recipients. We are the application. We are living epistles of His grace (2 Cor. 3:12). Conversely, ingratitude stems from a toxic "entitlement" spirit that presumes we are deserving. Often our times of prosperity feed into this. We see this in the account of Moses warning the children of Israel of what would happen when they made it to the promised land: "Then you say in your heart, 'My power and the might of my hand have gained me this wealth'" (Deut 8:17). This lack of gratitude ultimately led Israel into devastation.

Mercy and grace, however, remind us that God owes us nothing! We bring nothing to the table except our sin and brokenness. He doesn't need us, yet He loves us intensely with an everlasting love and new morning mercies. The prophet Jeremiah reminds us, "Through the Lord's mercies we are not consumed, because His compassions fail not. They are new every morning; great is Your faithfulness" (Lam. 3:22–23).

Grace can't be earned. Salvation can't be bought—except by the infinite price paid by our Redeemer. It's all of grace. "For by grace you have been saved through faith, and that not of yourselves; it is the gift of God, not of works, lest anyone should boast" (Eph. 2:8–9).

And this is what God has done concerning *you*. His grace has been applied to *us*. *We* are the blessed beneficiaries. In turn, we become His very expressions of grace to a lost, ungracious world. God has hugged us eternally in Christ Jesus. How can we not hug him back in thanksgiving?

Thanks-Living and the Author of 5:18

Did you know that the profound words in 1 Thessalonians 5:18 were penned by a man who suffered greatly and ended up in prison, alone and deserted? The apostle Paul actually wrote some of his letters while chained to a Roman guard. Our family has visited that very site, and it was pretty rough. Here's how each of the 5 A's of 5:18 brightly radiated from his life:

AMOUNT: As pain racked his body and blood flowed from his wounds, thanksgiving resided in his heart and resounded from his words. Paul gave thanks—even for his chains. Just look at the list of hardships he records in 2 Corinthians 11:

> Are they ministers of Christ?—I speak as a fool—I am more: in labors more abundant, in stripes above measure, in prisons more frequently, in deaths often. From the Jews five times I received forty stripes minus one. Three times I was beaten with rods; once I was stoned; three times I was shipwrecked; a night and a day I have been in the deep; in journeys often, in perils of waters, in perils of robbers, in perils of my own countrymen, in perils of the Gentiles, in perils in the city, in perils in the wilderness, in perils in the sea, in perils among false brethren; in weariness and toil, in sleeplessness often, in hunger and thirst, in fasting often, in cold and nakedness—besides the other things, what comes upon me daily: my deep concern for all the churches. Who is weak, and I am not weak? Who is made to stumble, and I do not burn with indignation? If I must boast, I will boast in

> the things which concern my infirmity. The God and Father of our Lord Jesus Christ, who is blessed forever, knows that I am not lying. In Damascus the governor, under Aretas the king, was guarding the city of the Damascenes with a garrison, desiring to arrest me; but I was let down in a basket through a window in the wall, and escaped from his hands. (vv. 11:23–33)

ACTION: In Paul's living and writing, he actively gave thanks. He exhorted his readers to live lives of grace and gratitude. He left no room for idle chat or idle living. After being severally beaten and bound by stocks in a dark cell in Philippi, Paul and Silas prayed and sang thanks to God. (Acts 16:25)

AIM: Nothing was more central to Paul's life than the will of God. He caught it, sought it, taught it, and lived it. His words in Romans 12:1–2 have become some of the most cited and taught verses in the entire New Testament. For Paul, God's will is his union with Him and that is the goal toward which Paul strives. Because God is "hugging" him, Paul hugs back with all his might.

ACCESS: Paul's Christology drove his doxology. Being found "in Him" was the basis of Paul's identity, lifestyle, and thanksgiving. He knew firsthand the grace from which the gratitude came. He recognized that the living water Himself, Jesus Christ, gives us grace leading to gratitude. He championed "grace and gratitude" until his final days on earth. Because Christ is in us, we have access to God and our true selves.

APPLICATION: Who better to apply the rich grace of Christ through a grateful life lived out by the saint? Most of Paul's writings open with the rich doctrines of grace. His epistles almost always conclude with gritty application culminating in gratitude. To the point where he even says in 2 Corinthians 3:2–3, "we are living epistles." When people read about the life of Paul and his disciples, they can't help but read "gratitude" all over the pages.

Five Traits of Thanksgiving

Second Corinthians, chapters 1 through 5 give us five rich characteristics of thankfulness as His redeemed children:

The first one is the "smell test" found in 2 Corinthians 2:15–16:

> For we are to God the fragrance of Christ among those who are being saved and among those who are perishing. To the one we are the aroma of death leading to death, and to the other the aroma of life leading to life. And who is sufficient for these things?

Do you pass the smell test? Are you an aroma of grace? Do you give off the odor of thanksgiving?

Then there's the "spell test" of 2 Corinthians 3:2–3:

> You are our epistle written in our hearts, known and read by all men; clearly you are an epistle of Christ, ministered by us, written not with ink but by the Spirit of the living God, not on tablets of stone but on tablets of flesh, that is, of the heart.

Do you pass the spell test? Are you an epistle of grace? What kind of thanksgiving book is your life writing for all to read?

Then we have the "veil test" of 2 Corinthians 3:18:

> But we all, with unveiled face, beholding as in a mirror the glory of the Lord, are being transformed into the same image from glory to glory, just as by the Spirit of the Lord.

Do you pass the veil test? Are you beholding and reflecting His glory with a thankful heart? Do you have His glory shining in your life? Are you glowing with gratitude like the one leper who returned to thank the Lord (Luke 17:11–19)?

Then we see the "shell test" in 2 Corinthians 4:7:

> But we have this treasure in earthen vessels, that the excellence of the power may be of God and not of us.

Do you pass the shell test? Are you grateful for being in Christ? Are you thankful that you have the divine deposit of the Holy Spirit of God in your earthly vessel? Do you gratefully acknowledge your utter dependence on Him? How does your thankfulness get expressed even in struggle? Are you weak, so He can be strong in your life?

The apostle climactically brings all of these exhortations to find their ultimate expression in thanksgiving in 4:15:

> For all things are for your sakes, that grace, having spread through the many, may cause thanksgiving to abound to the glory of God.

But wait, there's one more . . . the "tell test." Grateful hearts changed by the gospel can't help but share the truth with others. Our message, as "new creations" in Christ and "ambassadors for Christ," is simple: "Be reconciled to God" (2 Cor. 5:17–20).

While most born-again believers agree that they should actively share the gospel, the share of those who actually do so leaves much room for improvement.[3] I don't mention this to shame you, but to remind you of the glorious privilege we have to share the truth with others. Why shouldn't we be ambitious in sharing this great treasure? True thanksgiving will have gospel legs.

The good news isn't about my life, but about the life of Jesus. It's His perfect life and His perfect atoning death, burial, and resurrection that first brought thanksgiving to my soul (1 Cor. 15:1–4). A thankful heart can't help but share this good news with others. "The fruit of the righteous is a tree of life, and he who wins souls is wise" (Prov. 11:30).

Sharing the Gospel

My friend Jesse is thankful for God's work in his life and is one of the most enthusiastic evangelists I've ever known. Recently, we teamed up to start a new website, radio program, and podcast that mobilizes the people of God to share the truth out of a thankful heart. It's all on a simple card you can order for free. The website is ShareTheTruthNow.com. (We got the idea at Dad's funeral.) There is a QR code at the back of this book to help you order all the cards you want. Give them to those who are, as my friend Pastor Kyle always says, "close to you, but far from God."

In the same passage quoted earlier, Paul reminds us of the greatest application we have received. Christ's righteousness came to us in place of our sin: "For He made Him who knew no sin to be sin for us, that we might become the righteousness of God in Him" (2 Cor. 5:21).

Jesus Christ makes all this possible. As recipients of His grace, we are eternally blessed! Cicero rightly said, "Gratitude is the parent of all other virtues."[4] Our lives, therefore, should be marked by an attitude of gratitude. When's the last time you sent someone a thank-you text or a handwritten thank-you note? Take up your pen. Take up some paper. Pick up your phone. Pray first. Then, begin to write. What do you start with? Start with the two words "Thank you." My goal is to send one or two handwritten thank-you notes each week. Something about beginning with those two simple words loosens my pen and my thoughts.

Be thoughtful and intentional as you do this. Seize the grand opportunity to be a blessing to others. Include a Scripture verse.

Do those around me perceive these inspired words when they see my life and hear me speak? Are they witnessing thanksgiving applied? Am I a walking, talking, "Thank You, Jesus" sign? Am I giving thanks in everything because it is God's will in Christ? Do others see that I have been marked by Jesus? Am I an advertisement for the glory and grandeur of God?

At some point, someone, somehow, somewhere is going to inquire, "Who is he giving thanks to? What is she giving thanks for? And why is he always thankful?" It's another open door to tell people all about our Jesus.

Recently, my late father was recognized at a special dinner by some well-known people. My mom was invited to receive an award in his honor. She stepped up to the podium, and once again, set a blessed tone with these words:

> Before Stu went to heaven, I always worried about how difficult it would be dealing with his death. But the most amazing thing has happened. Not only did God give Stu dying grace, but He has also poured out His amazing grace on me in this season. It's like He's given me survivor's grace. I have felt overwhelmed by gratitude and joy to my Lord for the sixty wonderful years I had with Stu. God's grace has truly been sufficient! Best of all, because of the great hope of the resurrection, we know we'll all see him again.

The room erupted in applause. The blessing of thanksgiving was poured out on everyone there.

This raises the question: How am *I* seizing every opportunity, even at someone's homegoing, to thankfully share the good news of what He gave me? The application doesn't stop with you; it comes *to* you to flow *through* you to bless others.

How have these five A's spoken to you?

- The Amount—How often are you thankful?
- The Action—How are you actively giving thanks regardless of feelings or circumstances?
- The Aim—How has connecting to God and His will resulted in a heart of thanksgiving?

- The Access—Is your heart full of thanks for the One who purchased you with His precious blood and brought you into fellowship with God?
- The Application—How thankful are you for all the eternal benefits you have freely received as a beloved child of God in union with Christ?

As you consider your answers to these questions, will you join me in this prayer—quietly—before God?

> Lord, I confess when I've been blind to all the blessings You've bestowed upon me in Christ. Forgive me for being an ungrateful taker. Thank You for giving me the gift of salvation in Christ, for saving me and making me Your child. Whether during the Thanksgiving season or any other time of year, please open the eyes of my heart to see thanksgiving as I've never seen it before. Give me a deeper appreciation for the supernatural work of grace You have done for me in the gospel. Show me how I can share this good news with others. In Jesus' name, amen.

Preparing for the King's Return

Our great King is returning. In His first coming, Jesus finished His perfect work to make us His sons and daughters. In His second coming, He will take us home. May we be found not merely faithful, but let us also be found *thankful.* May we, with grateful hearts, share the good news with our lost world. For a world without Christ is a world ultimately with *nothing* to be thankful for:

> For to everyone who has, more will be given, and he will have abundance; but from him who does not have, even what he has will be taken away. (Matt. 25:29)

> And how shall they preach unless they are sent? As it is written: "How beautiful are the feet of those who preach the gospel of peace, who bring glad tidings of good things!" (Rom. 10:15)

By contrast, Paul's encouraging words to the young Thessalonian church two millennia ago—and to us—still ring true. Our life of thanksgiving looks forward to the triumphal return of King Jesus. Justice and peace, which we experience now only in part, will reign completely in the new heaven and new earth. This time, the Lord won't be facing trial and execution. He will execute judgment on His enemies and bring ultimate salvation to His elect. He'll establish His kingdom, and we will reign with Him forever.

Are *you* ready for that great day? He *will* be praised. He *will* receive thanks. The heavens declare His glory. The rocks are ready to cry out. Will *you* thank Him? In *everything*? Are you living for God? Have you received the salvation that is only in Christ Jesus? Do you realize the treasure trove of blessings God offers you?

Thanksgiving and praise on earth are but a brief rehearsal for the glories of eternity and the great thanksgiving feasts of heaven when our faith becomes sight:

> And every creature which is in heaven and on the earth and under the earth and such as are in the sea, and all that are in them, I heard saying:

> "Blessing and honor and glory and power
> Be to Him who sits on the throne,
> And to the Lamb, forever and ever!" (Rev. 5:13)

Thank You, Jesus, that You're coming again! Let me be found praising You on that day.

Living thanks and thanks-living could mean spending most of your life in a wheelchair, yet being ever thankful that you are in the middle of His perfect will. Joni Eareckson Tada, a quadriplegic since she was seventeen, said that she wants to take her wheelchair to heaven:

> I sure hope I can bring this wheelchair to heaven. Now, I know that's not theologically correct. But I hope to bring it and put it in a little corner of heaven, and then in my new, perfect, glorified body, standing on grateful glorified legs, I'll stand next to my Savior, holding his nail-pierced hands.
>
> I'll say, "Thank you, Jesus," and he will know that I mean it, because he knows me.
>
> He'll recognize me from the fellowship we're now sharing in his sufferings.
>
> And I will say, "Jesus do you see that wheelchair? You were right when you said that in this world we would have trouble, because that thing was a lot of trouble. But the weaker I was in that thing, the harder I leaned on you. And the harder I leaned on you, the stronger I discovered you to be. It never would have happened had you not given

> me the bruising of the blessing of that wheelchair."
>
> Then the real ticker-tape parade of praise will begin. And all of earth will join the party.
>
> And at that point Christ will open up our eyes to the great fountain of joy in his heart for us beyond all that we ever experienced on earth.
>
> And when we're able to stop laughing and crying, the Lord Jesus will wipe away our tears.
>
> I find it so poignant that finally, at the point when I do have the use of my arms to wipe away my own tears, I won't have to, because God will.[5]

Let's grab a pen and our Thanksgiving journal and start by writing down one thing we are thankful for. Someone has greatly impacted your life. What a blessing it will be for them to receive a note, text, visit, or a phone call with a simple "thank you." Don't wait for the eulogy—do it today! Let us pray daily that the grace of gratitude will drop from our heads to our hearts to our feet . . . going with us everywhere we go. May our thanksgiving become thanks-living. As you allow yourself to be held by His embrace, you will find yourself embracing the power of gratitude every day.

Discussion Questions for Chapter 7

1. What basic gifts am I thankful for? (e.g. a roof over my head, oxygen, food, plumbing, family.)
2. What deeper spiritual things am I thankful for? Salvation, adoption, spiritual gifts, heaven, forgiveness, others?
3. How does being thankful eliminate pride, idle talk, worry, and coarse jesting?
4. How can I share these 5:18 truths with my family?

Living Thanks . . . Write It Down

5. What has this chapter inspired me to record in my gratitude journal?
6. Write a list of people to whom I could send a small thank-you gift.
7. To whom can I write a thank-you note for giving me wisdom and guidance at a pivotal time in my life?

APPENDIX 1

Thanksgiving Scriptures

"Oh, give thanks to the Lord!
Call upon His name;
Make known His deeds among the peoples!"
(1 Chron.16:8)

"And they sang responsively, praising and giving thanks to the Lord:
'For He is good,
For His mercy endures forever toward Israel.'
Then all the people shouted with a great shout, when they praised the Lord, because the foundation of the house of the Lord was laid."
(Ezra 3:11)

"I will praise You, O Lord, with my whole heart;
I will tell of all Your marvelous works."
(Ps. 9:1)

"I will sing to the LORD,
Because He has dealt bountifully with me."
(Ps. 13:6)

"Therefore I will give thanks to You, O LORD, among the Gentiles,
And sing praises to Your name."
(Ps. 18:49)

"That I may proclaim with the voice of thanksgiving,
And tell of all Your wondrous works."
(Ps. 26:7)

"The LORD is my strength and my shield;
My heart trusted in Him, and I am helped;
Therefore my heart greatly rejoices,
And with my song I will praise Him."
(Ps. 28:7)

"Sing praise to the LORD, you saints of His,
And give thanks at the remembrance of His holy name."
(Ps. 30:4)

"I will bless the LORD at all times;
His praise shall continually be in my mouth."
(Ps. 34:1)

"Sing praises to God, sing praises!
Sing praises to our King, sing praises!"
(Ps. 47:6)

"Whoever offers praise glorifies Me;
And to him who orders his conduct aright
I will show the salvation of God."
(Ps. 50:23)

"Because Your lovingkindness is better than life,
My lips shall praise You."
(Ps. 63:3)

"We give thanks to You, O God, we give thanks!
For Your wondrous works declare that Your name is near."
(Ps. 75:1)

"It is good to give thanks to the Lord,
And to sing praises to Your name, O Most High;
To declare Your lovingkindness in the morning,
And Your faithfulness every night."
(Ps. 92:1–2)

"Rejoice in the Lord, you righteous,
And give thanks at the remembrance of His holy name."
(Ps. 97:12)

"Enter into His gates with thanksgiving,
And into His courts with praise.
Be thankful to Him, and bless His name."
(Ps. 100:4)

"Oh, give thanks to the LORD!
Call upon His name;
Make known His deeds among the peoples!"
(Ps. 105:1)

"Oh, give thanks to the LORD, for He is good!
For His mercy endures forever."
(Ps. 107:1)

"Let them sacrifice the sacrifices of thanksgiving,
And declare His works with rejoicing."
(Ps. 107:22)

"I will offer to You the sacrifice of thanksgiving,
And will call upon the name of the LORD."
(Ps. 116:17)

"Oh, give thanks to the LORD, for He is good! For His mercy endures forever."
(Ps. 118:1)

"My lips shall utter praise,
For You teach me Your statutes."
(Ps. 119:171)

"When the Lord brought back the captivity of Zion..
We were like those who dream,
Then our mouth was filled with laughter,
And our tongue with singing,

Then they said among the nations,
"The Lord has done great things for them,
The Lord has done great things for us,
And we are glad."
Psalm 126:1-3

"Oh, give thanks to the God of gods!
For His mercy endures forever.
Oh, give thanks to the Lord of lords!
For His mercy endures forever
Oh, give thanks to the God of heaven!
For His mercy endures forever."
(Ps. 136:2–3, 26)

"I will praise You with my whole heart;
Before the gods I will sing praises to You.
I will worship toward Your holy temple,
And praise Your name
For Your lovingkindness and Your truth;
For You have magnifies Your word above all Your name.
In the day when I cried out, You answered me,
And made me bold with strength in my soul.

All the kings of the earth shall praise You, O Lord,
When they hear the words of Your mouth.
Yes, they shall sing of the ways of the Lord,
For great is the glory of the Lord.

Though the Lord is on high,
Yet He regards the lowly;
But the proud He knows from afar.

Though I walk in the midst of trouble, You will revive me;
You will stretch out Your hand
Against the wrath of my enemies,
And Your right hand will save me.
The Lord will perfect that which concerns me;
Your mercy, O Lord, endures forever;
Do not forsake the works of Your hands.
(Ps. 138)

"I will praise You, for I am fearfully and wonderfully made;
Marvelous are Your works,
And that my soul knows very well."
(Ps. 139:14)

"My mouth shall speak the praise of the LORD,
And all flesh shall bless His holy name
Forever and ever."
(Ps. 145:21)

"While I live I will praise the LORD;
I will sing praises to my God while I have my being."
(Ps. 146:2)

"Let everything that has breath praise the LORD.
Praise the LORD!"
(Ps. 150:6)

"But I will sacrifice to You
With the voice of thanksgiving;
I will pay what I have vowed.
Salvation is of the LORD."
(Jonah 2:9)

"Then He took the cup, and gave thanks, and gave it to them, saying, 'Drink from it, all of you.'"
(Matt. 26:27)

"So He commanded the multitude to sit down on the ground. And He took the seven loaves and gave thanks, broke them and gave them to His disciples to set before them; and they set them before the multitude."
(Mark 8:6)

"And coming in that instant she gave thanks to the Lord, and spoke of Him to all those who looked for redemption in Jerusalem."
(Luke 2:38)

"Then He took the cup, and gave thanks, and said, 'Take this and divide it among yourselves.'"
(Luke 22:17)

"And when he had said these things, he took bread and gave thanks to God in the presence of them all; and when he had broken it he began to eat."
(Acts 27:35)

"But thanks be to God, who gives us the victory through our Lord Jesus Christ."
(1 Cor. 15:57)

"Now thanks be to God who always leads us in triumph in Christ, and through us diffuses the fragrance of His knowledge in every place."
(2 Cor. 2:14)

"For all things are for your sakes, that grace, having spread through the many, may cause thanksgiving to abound to the glory of God."
(2 Cor. 4:15)

"While you are enriched in everything for all liberality, which causes thanksgiving through us to God."
(2 Cor. 9:11)

"Thanks be to God for His indescribable gift!"
(2 Cor. 9:15)

"Neither filthiness, nor foolish talking, nor coarse jesting, which are not fitting, but rather giving of thanks."
(Eph. 5:4)

"Giving thanks always for all things to God the Father in the name of our Lord Jesus Christ."
(Eph. 5:20)

"Be anxious for nothing, but in everything by prayer and supplication, with thanksgiving, let your requests be made known to God."
(Phil. 4:6)

"Rooted and built up in Him and established in the faith, as you have been taught, abounding in it with thanksgiving."
(Col. 2:7)

"And let the peace of God rule in your hearts, to which also you were called in one body; and be thankful."
(Col. 3:15)

"And whatever you do in word or deed, do all in the name of the Lord Jesus, giving thanks to God the Father through Him."
(Col. 3:17)

"Continue earnestly in prayer, being vigilant in it with thanksgiving."
(Col. 4:2)

"For every creature of God is good, and nothing is to be refused if it is received with thanksgiving."
(1 Tim. 4:4)

"Therefore by Him let us continually offer the sacrifice of praise to God, that is, the fruit of our lips, giving thanks to His name." (Heb. 13:15)

"Saying:
'Amen! Blessing and glory and wisdom,
Thanksgiving and honor and power and might,
Be to our God forever and ever.
Amen.'"
(Rev. 7:12)

APPENDIX 2

5 A's of 5:18 Song

In everything give thanks
In everything give thanks . . .
For this is the will of God in Christ concerning you . . . in everything give thanks, in everything give thanks . . . For this is the will of God in Christ concerning you . . .
The Amount is . . . everything
The Action is . . . giving thanks
The will of God is . . . our highest aim
The Access comes through Jesus Christ.
Who paid the greatest price . . .
He gave everything . . . and we give thanks

In everything give thanks
In everything give thanks . . .
For this is the will of God in Christ concerning you . . .
In everything give thanks . . .

In everything give thanks . . . For this is the will of God in Christ concerning you . . .

He lived full of truth and grace . . .
He suffered and died in my place . . .
He conquered death and rose from the grave . . .
Someday He'll return again and we shall see His face . . .
He gave everything . . . so we give thanks . . .

In everything give thanks . . .
In everything give thanks . . .
For this is the will of God in Christ concerning you . . .
In everything give thanks . . .
In everything give thanks . . .
For this is the will of God in Christ concerning you.[1]

APPENDIX 3

Count Your Blessings[1]

Johnson Oatman Jr. was a bivocational pastor who wrote more than five thousand songs. He's best known for the classic "Count Your Blessings." The beautiful lyrics are below. His song, and the motivation behind it, prove the incompatibility of ingratitude and faith. It's impossible to be thankful and, at the same time, be grumpy, cantankerous, critical, or ill-tempered. That's a lesson Oatman wanted to teach young people.[2]

When upon life's billows you are tempest-tossed,
When you are discouraged, thinking all is lost,
Count your many blessings, name them one by one,
And it will surprise you what the Lord has done.

Refrain:
Count your blessings, name them one by one,
Count your blessings, see what God has done!
Count your blessings, name them one by one,

*Count your many blessings, see what God has done.
[*And it will surprise you what the Lord has done.]

Are you ever burdened with a load of care?
Does the cross seem heavy you are called to bear?
Count your many blessings, every doubt will fly,
And you will keep singing as the days go by.

When you look at others with their lands and gold,
Think that Christ has promised you His wealth untold;
Count your many blessings—*money cannot buy [*wealth can never buy]
Your reward in heaven, nor your home on high.

So, amid the conflict whether great or small,
Do not be discouraged, God is over all;
Count your many blessings, angels will attend,
Help and comfort give you to your journey's end.

*alternate text

Acknowledgments

This book was born out of a simple study of God's Word. At first, I couldn't let go of this one little verse. Then, it wouldn't let go of me. I've taught or written this material off and on for over six years. Mom's remarkable response to our pastor the day Dad went to heaven pushed me over the top. I'm praying that there may be more of these "one verse wonder" books ahead.

I'm so grateful for godly parents who exposed me to solid Bible teaching all of my life. Much gratitude goes to my sweet (and patient) wife, Julie, along with our four daughters Hope, Gracie, Joy, and Faith. My son-in-law, Harrison; grandsons Walker and Watson, who supported me all the way through, as well as the rest of my siblings, nephews, and nieces.

Big kudos to Stan Guthrie, an all-star wordsmith who tightened it up to get it ready for publishing. Team Moody has been wonderful all the way: John Hinkley on point; Amanda Cleary Eastep with exceptional editing; and Erica, Janis, Kaylee, and Steve in their tremendous creative/marketing/launch efforts. Wonderful to work with such a well-focused and seasoned team that kept me on track all the way through.

Special thanks to some sage proofreaders and writing mentors: Dr. Chapman, Uncle Ray, Coach Hank, Jason, Sanger, Double J, Dr. Null, Uncle Dwight, Mom, and Auntie Mo.

My Wednesday in the Word brothers and Women in the Word sisters have been tremendous cheerleaders ever since they first heard this material several years ago at Dairio. Jamaal blessed me with a thanks-giving tie that I've enjoyed wearing at random times of the year, just to provoke everyone toward thanks-living!

Grateful for Ballernation and all my basketball family out there. Thank you for graciously listening to all my sweaty thanks-living devos and prayers. Keep shining His light of gratitude on and off the court.

Truth Network family, you give me so much to be thankful for: Jamie with all the edits, the Christian Car Guy, Boss Lady, the moms of the light, and everyone else helping spread the word across the airwaves.

Notes

Dedication

1. "Service for Stu Epperson Sr.," Calvary Now, July 24, 2023, https://youtube.com/watch?v=cHN5X3C8qEs&feature=sharea.

Chapter 1: Thanks-Living: Why 5:18?

1. Epigraph: Jerry Bridges, *Transforming Grace* (NavPress, 2017), 230.
2. Jamal, a faithful member from our Wednesday in the Word men's group, blessed me with a Thanksgiving necktie last year. Yes, it's attracted some strange looks and comments in July and September. But the more I've studied 5:18, the more emboldened I've been to wear it at random times of the year and not just in November. Thank you, Jamal!
3. "US Public Becoming Less Religious," Pew Research Center, November 3, 2015, https://www.pewresearch.org/religion/2015/11/03/u-s-public-becoming-less-religious/.
4. Robert Emmons, "Why Gratitude Is Good," *Greater Good* magazine, November 16, 2010, https://greatergood.berkeley.edu/article/item/why_gratitude_is_good.
5. Ibid.
6. Ibid.
7. Ibid.
8. Mark Hyman, MD, @drmarkhyman X post, "Gratitude is the ultimate biohack," November 28, 2024, https://x.com/drmarkhyman/status/1862135859845415036.
9. Quoted in Stephen Nichols, "What Is Thanksgiving Day?," Ligonier Ministries, November 23, 2020, https://www.ligonier.org/learn/articles/what-is-thanksgiving-day.

Chapter 2: Setting the 5:18 Table

1. Epigraph: Nancy DeMoss Wolgemuth, "The Invitation of a Lifetime," quoted in Deeper Christian Quotes, December 14, 2020, https://deeperchristianquotes.com/the-invitation-of-a-lifetime-nancy-demoss-wolgemuth/.
2. For more on Corrie's story, see Stan Guthrie, *Victorious: Corrie ten Boom and The Hiding Place* (2019).
3. Jack Hayford, *The Spirit-Filled Life Study Bible* (Thomas Nelson, 2018).
4. John Piper, "How Do You Define Joy?," *Desiring God*, July 25, 2015, https://www.desiringgod.org/articles/how-do-you-define-joy.
5. "1 Thessalonians 5:17 Commentary," Precept Austin, https://www.preceptaustin.org/1_thessalonians_517_commentary#:~:text=The%20practical%20demands%20of%20life,of%20prayer%20should%20be%20incessant.
6. Charles A. Wanamaker, *The Epistles to the Thessalonians* (Eerdmans, 1929), 65.
7. Chip Ingram, "Worship: The Key to Drawing Near to God," Crosswalk, November 12, 2007, https://www.crosswalk.com/church/worship/worship-the-key-to-drawing-near-to-god-11559086.html.
8. Matthew Henry Commentary on 1 Thessalonians. 1 Thessalonians 5, https://www.biblestudytools.com/commentaries/matthew-henry-complete/1-thessalonians/5.html. Emphasis added.
9. Wanamaker, *The Epistles to the Thessalonians*, 65.

Chapter 3: The Amount—"In Everything"

1. Epigraph: C. S. Lewis, "1459 Thanksgiving, Letters: C. S. Lewis/Don Giovanni Calabria (10 August 1948)," The Quotable Lewis, eds. Wayne Martindale and Jerry Root (Tyndale, 1990), 579.
2. https://5lovelanguages.com/learn. See also, "Gary Chapman (author)," Wikipedia, https://en.wikipedia.org/wiki/Gary_Chapman_(author).
3. Used by permission.
4. H. U. Westermayer, quoted in *The Newton Bee*, November 24, 2009, https://www.newtownbee.com/11242009/the-pilgrims-made-seven-times-more-graves-than-huts-no-americans-have-been/.
5. *Great Preaching on Thanksgiving*, compiled by Curtis Hutson (Sword of the Lord Publishing, 1987), 15.
6. J. I. Packer, quoted in Matt Smethurst, "40 Quotes from J. I. Packer (1926–2020)," The Gospel Coalition, July 17, 2024, https://www.thegospelcoalition.org/article/40-quotes-from-j-i-packer/.
7. "Joni Eareckson Tada on Wilberforce Award, 'Better Off Dead Than Disabled' Mentality,'" interview with Eryn Sun, March 16, 2012, www.christianpost.com.

8. Read the entire remarkable account in Dr. Chapman's book *Life Lessons and Love Languages: What I've Learned on My Unexpected Journey* (Moody, 2021).

Chapter 4: The Action—"Give Thanks"

1. Epigraph: A. W. Tozer (1897–1963) as recounted by Vernon K. McLellan, *Twentieth Century Thoughts That Shaped the Church* (Tyndale House, 2000) 242.
2. Quoted in Burk Parsons, "The Heart of John Calvin," Ligonier Ministries, July 10, 2019, https://www.ligonier.org/learn/articles/heart-john-calvin.
3. Woodrow M. Kroll, quoted in AZ Quotes, https://www.azquotes.com/author/22604-Woodrow_M_Kroll.
4. William Shakespeare, *King Lear*, Act I, scene 4, lines 815–16.
5. *Great Preaching on Thanksgiving*, compiled by Curtis Hutson (Sword of the Lord Publishing, 1987), 87.
6. "Lexicon: Strong's G5483 charizomai," Blue Letter Bible, https://www.blueletterbible.org/lexicon/g5483/kjv/tr/0-1/.
7. Ben Patterson, "Deepening Your Conversation with God," quoted in Nancy Kay Grace, "What's the Difference Between Praise and Thanks?," https://www.nancykaygrace.com/praise-thanks-difference/.
8. Isaac Watts, "Come, Thou Fount of Every Blessing," Hymnary, https://hymnary.org/text/come_thou_fount_of_every_blessing.
9. Dietrich Bonhoeffer, *Letters and Papers from Prison* (Simon and Schuster, 2011), 52.

Chapter 5: The Aim—"This Is the Will of God"

1. Epigraph: Kay Arthur, quoted in Our Daily Verse, https://www.ourdailyverse.com/p/verse-day-romans-828-71fe.
2. "Shorter Catechism: Text and Scripture Proofs," The Westminster Standard, https://thewestminsterstandard.org/westminster-shorter-catechism/.
3. Nancy Leigh DeMoss, *A Place of Quiet Rest: Finding Intimacy with God Through a Daily Devotional Life* (Moody, 2017), 70.

Chapter 6: The Access—"In Christ Jesus"

1. Epigraph: John Ortberg, *When the Game Is Over, It All Goes Back in the Box* (Zondervan, 2007), 149.
2. "Lexicon: Strong's G5485 charis," Blue Letter Bible, https://www.blueletterbible.org/lexicon/g5485/kjv/tr/0-1/.
3. Gene Veith, "Thanksgiving Days and Thanksgiving Feasts in the Bible," *Cranach: The Blog of Veith*, November 22, 2017, https://www.patheos.com/blogs/geneveith/2017/11/thanksgiving-days-and-thanksgiving-feasts-in-the-bible/.

4. David Jeremiah, *The Jeremiah Study Bible, NKJV: What It Says. What It Means. What It Means For You* (Worthy Books, 2013), 90.
5. Ibid.
6. Tom Holland, *Dominion: How the Christian Revolution Remade the World* (Basic Books, 2019), 540–41.
7. J. I. Packer and Carolyn Nystrom, *Knowing God Devotional Journal: A One-Year Guide* (InterVarsity Press, 2009), 231.

Chapter 7: The Application—"Concerning You"

1. Epigraph: A. W. Pink, "Rejoice in the Lord Alway," O. Christian.com, http://articles.ochristian.com/article710.shtml.
2. Used by permission of Robby Dilmore.
3. "An April 2022 Evangelism Explosion study conducted by Lifeway Research found that less than half of self-identified Christians have, at least once in the past six months, shared a Bible verse or Bible story with a non-Christian loved one (46 percent), invited a non-Christian friend or family member to attend a church service or other program at church (43 percent), or shared with a non-Christian loved one how to become a Christian (38 percent). The same study also identified that almost 2 in 3 Christians (65 percent) agree sharing with a nonbeliever how they can become a Christian is the most loving thing they can do for them." See Kent E. Fillinger, "Evangelism Matters!," *Christian Standard*, November 1, 2023, https://christianstandard.com/2023/11/evangelism-matters/.
4. Quoted in Stanley Ly, MA, LPC, "Gratitude, the Parent of All Virtues," University of Colorado Boulder, April 29, 2020, https://www.colorado.edu/hr/2020/04/29/gratitude-parent-all-virtues#:~:text=Roman%20philosopher%20Cicero%20is%20sourced,paler%2C%20hollowed%2C%20and%20less%20inspired.
5. Excerpt from Joni Eareckson Tada, "Hope . . . the Best of Things" (Good News Publishers, 2008), quoted in Randy Alcorn, "Joni Eareckson Tada on Suffering, Sorrow, Wheelchairs and Eternal Gratitude," Eternal Perspective Ministries, November 7, 2016, https://www.epm.org/resources/2016/Nov/7/joni-suffering-sorrow-wheelchairs/.

Appendix 2

1. Lyrics by Stu Epperson.

Appendix 3

1. Johnson Oatman Jr., "Count Your Blessings" (lyrics), 1897, public domain, https://library.timelesstruths.org/music/Count_Your_Blessings/.
2. Robert Morgan, *Then Sings My Soul* (Thomas Nelson, 2011), 243.